THOUGHTS ON AN ARCHITECT'S JOURNEY

Open Notes at 85

JAN WAMPLER

For Liz,
my companion, editor,
friend and deep love
over the years

THOUGHTS ON AN ARCHITECT'S JOURNEY

Open Notes at 85

Text Jan Wampler
Foreword Aldo Van Eyck, John Habraken, Fumihiko Maki
Comment Robert M. MacLeod
Interview Paul Lukez

JAN WAMPLER

OSCAR RIERA OJEDA
PUBLISHERS

CONTENTS

FOREWORD

ALDO VAN EYCK

Deceased 1999

From Open Strings for E Exhibition and Publication at MIT

What Jan Wampler brings to bear here is the plain truth: truth of a kind most people – architects among them – wish not to hear and therefore soon brush aside. The sound is clear enough, but what about echo?

In this great, socially not yet completely developed country you could, thirty years ago, come across individuals of a sort now probably extinct. I am lucky and satisfied to cherish just one of them as a close friend. It started on Massachusetts Avenue where a small vehicle – straps and strings literally holding it together – picked me up. The driver and the vehicle were as one: the former's hair was everywhere – blowing in the wind and so, it soon appeared were the notions in his head, which no faculty of architecture or planning was willing to tune in on. Not until Dean Jose Sert said OK, disregarding all formal entry requirements. From that enlightened gesture the entire architecture department benefited, Sert told me afterwards. The very same notions, extended and ripened, are gathered together here now. The need is still the same – overwhelmingly so – also the implicit message. The trouble, however, is that it would take legions of Jan Wampler's sort to turn the course of architecture and sought-after architects not to lose sight altogether of their profession's ultimate purpose, which is basically down-to-earth and obvious, like the general practitioner's or baker's just up the road: i.e. to build as well as you can for the benefit of "PEOPLE"; meaning at least in spirit, "ALL" people.

Meanwhile lots of other notions – nasty ones – have taken hold of far too many architects, nudging them in the wrong direction, like the outrageous idea that architecture requires no social or human justification to be viable. On the contrary, once liberated from such ballast and rendered "autonomous" it will be at last be allowed, they hope, to serve no other than its original purpose, which is to constitute ART – BUILT art.

So now we have architect/artists all over the world contriving useless artifacts, which look more or less like buildings. At the same time we have Jan Wampler striking a discord, albeit a sane one, by suggesting that buildings should be useful and built for the benefit of, I repeat, ALL – not some – people. "Autonomous" architecture is therefore just another ugly contradiction in terms. That is the hard and simple truth from which there is no acceptable escape. But, that is exactly where the trouble lies: good buildings haven't got what they needn't have and belong to where they are put. So "put" your heart into your pencil – or computer – and enjoy what you are doing, the way Jan does. This is his message. Himself a born artisan who turns – assembles – all he knows about people, construction, and materials (especially discarded ceramics and colored glass) into small, beautiful buildings. What you cannot learn from Las Vegas – ever – you can learn from them, and following the same line, from his moving book: *All Their Own: People and Places They Build*. The title sets the tone – which is what counts – as well as the opening paragraph, which I shall quote. Jan told me about places he loved like La Perla, San Juan, Puerto Rico, thirty years ago. I went to see that breathtaking achievement, made by people with their backs against the wall of poverty and barely able to parry the thrust of the sea so very close by.

I quote: There was a time in this country when the building of your home was common. The leaving of your mark or imprint on the land for your children and grandchildren – by making a farm, building a house or planting a tree – was the natural thing to do.

And written in my own words not long after we met: If behaving with sanity towards environment is no longer within our reach – within reach of societies – our kind – which behave towards the landscapes of the world like a half-wit with two left hands, then, surely, such societies, thus reasonably gauged, are of a low – "primitive" – order.

Whether in Greenland, Africa, America – long ago – or or the South Seas, people dealt with limited number both accurately and gracefully, extending collective behavior into adequate and often beautiful form. Taking from the environment as much as they gave, a gratifying balanced was sustained. This we are no longer able to do, not in the same way, nor as yet in any other way.

Yet, is it really all that difficult or beyond our reach? Do we not belong to the same species as those in Greenland, Africa, America – long ago – and the South Seas? Is our mental equipment not similar? Are we not endowed equally well? Surely we can accomplish what they accomplish in so many different ways. Believe it or not, those little societies and their fast disappearing cultures, can by their example still tell us that abilities (hence also possibilities) which we have come to regard as beyond the scope of human being actually lie within it. So, there is no reason to give up all hope. For it is in the nature of the human species – all people – to be able to deal with environment, hence also to fashion the spaces they require, adequately – and sometimes beautifully. The way people are also given to communicate with each other through language – speech – that other gift, which, like making spaces, still belongs to their primordial equipment.

It is painfully true of architecture that it is not just good quality that counts but a sufficient quantity of that quality. A good school elsewhere is no use to a child in need of one here. If I have a nice house, (a house at all), it does not mean that millions upon millions of others also do. So let's get moving bearing this in mind.

JOHN HABRAKEN

Deceased 2013
From Open Strings for E Exhibition and Publication at MIT
Revised August 15, 2014

Seeing Jan Wampler coming down the corridor
He moves like a person possessed;
spirits stirring soul and body

As he goes.
He takes in everything in a glance
(students, models, drawings, pin ups,
a room, a building, a landscape).
responding to it all with keen intelligence.

But at all times, the quick mind
is governed by the heart
which renders him vulnerable.

His buildings hug the land,
then rise from it:
roofs hovering in space like daffodils

He was born to the American heritage
of Thoreau, Whitman and Wright; to the
idea of reciprocity between man and nature
(the land nurturing people,
people working the land,
the building the fruit).

He has nursed that heritage
at his own pace, for years
following hidden channels,
guided by intuition,
and memories of human dignity.

And now he makes it bloom in unexpected ways:
In the recognition of the urban fabric
(woven from space, mostly)
as a landscape of another kind.
To be settled in
and to grow buildings from.

And in the villages of foreign countries,
where people build like birds do,
because birth, feeding, loving, dying,
must happen someplace
to happen at all.

No grand plans, no abstractions;
local acts must prevail.

He goes unarmed,
seeks no power,
but does not step aside easily,

and has the courage to look truth in the face.

He does not exploit his talents
to personal advantage
and sets no goals to strive for,
but he moves like a person bound to task.

A task he only will understand when done
a bondage leaving him no time to waste.

FUMIHIKO MAKI
Deceased 2024
October 2014

I met Jan Wampler in the fall of 1964 when he was enrolled in the Urban Design program of the Graduate School of Design (GSD), Harvard University. My vivid memory of him at that time is of an intense, passionate young man, uncompromising in this position wherever discussion erupted around us. He fervently believed that the first order of an architect's task was to give his service to the betterment of our physical environment, primarily of cities, and that, in order to create meaningful places to live and work, an architect needed to be sensitive to people and culture.

To this end he has now devoted forty years of teaching, practice, and research, infusing into his work all his ideas, dreams and reflections. Through the many difficulties he faced during those years, he has never lost his warm heart or his humane capacity to understand the basic nature of our world. We have seen each other many times, the most recently at GSD in 2014, but it seems as though we have just met yesterday every time because he is always the same person, pursuing the goals he has set for himself.

I still cherish the memory of the time we shared together toward the end of academic year 1964-1965. With three other members of his class, we formed a special study group to investigate movement systems in the central district of Boston, postulating that the cross-points between different movement systems could become catalysts for generating a more humanistic public network for pedestrians. Ideas such as the "city-room" or "city-corridor" were born out of this study, for which he made a great contribution. Reading his recent remarks that the quality of a city "can be measured by its public spaces" I felt again this strong thread of continuity in his thoughts throughout his career.

We are said to be moving towards a global society – or in Marshall McLuhan's words, a global village; this does not mean, however, that places are becoming the same all over the world. We will still find discrete differences among many things we might consider at first to be the same and paradoxically, we could also find commonality among cultural artifacts we take for granted to be different. Only this awareness can lead us to creating cities and places with a sense of individual identity. Jan Wampler's work over the last forty years provides ample testimony to this ideal.

Ordinary people do not usually possess the means to express and translate their desires into physical reality. Often they do not even know what their hidden desires are. Wampler's approach to any given task is to first make a thorough reconnaissance of a place's history, geography, human and natural resources, customs and mores. Then, he begins dialogues with the dwellers, users and other related people to uncover their values and desires. Using his life-long structuralist discipline, he sensitively navigates his inquiry together with those involved. Through this process, a physical construct or image gradually begins to emerge.

All architecture, Wampler claims, is a life form. Along with the participatory efforts of the residents, it grows and changes over time like trees. What then is a sustainable community? A sustainable community must be a place where people can nurture their dreams for a better life in the future, both individually and collectively – no matter how modest.

Jan Wampler's work over the last forty years provides ample testimony to this ideal.

INTRODUCTION

Jan Wampler
July 2024
wampler@mit.edu

These are notes on my architectural work and my thoughts at 85, which I am now. I have no idea how that happened – only yesterday in my mind I was 8½ at my grandparents' farm. But here it is, and there is so much to do now, even more than before (whenever that was).

I want to design more buildings (my next one will be my best one), and it is so thrilling to visit a new site, like a Christmas morning. And then there are all the paintings I have not done; it's just so exciting to see them take life on paper or canvas. Then there are books to read, places to visit (I want to see Petra, the ancient rock-cut city in southern Jordan), sunsets to see, and, yes, my cello to play.

I played the cello for a while years ago, but I have never been good at practicing it. Actually, I hate practicing. For some time I had a cello mate, and each week we would meet and play, and I did have to practice for this, because, who wants to be the one that screws up the piece? Perhaps she felt the same. At first we played the same notes, and we often sounded good together. But then that became boring, so I would compose a piece for her to play. Sometimes she played the melody, sometimes I did. Then I would often write notes I thought might sound good together – and sometimes they did, other times they sounded awful. I had no idea what I was doing, but that did not stop me. I kept looking for some magical word or note, perhaps from above, though it never came. Then she moved away. It was horrible, I missed our times together, and I stopped practicing. Recently I proposed to a friend that we play together on Zoom, but it did not take to him. So now on my own I must practice every day.

I have much to do in all of the areas of my interest, and the work is getting more complicated. Perhaps I am getting more critical.

This book has several components. It begins with a substantial interview summing up my architectural work and the last 70 years of my life. Following the interview are visuals of my work, both architectural and painted. Verses, which I call "Soul Songs," conclude both the interview and the visuals. The Soul Songs are my memories and thoughts over the past year, some very personal to me, and some related to the condition of architecture.

These parts can be read separately. The interview, the visuals, and the Soul Songs will each tell the story of my work over the years. Of course, they can also be read continuously together, as a total statement about my architecture.

Most important, an essay by Robert MacLeod discusses my work at the University of South Florida, where I have taught for the last 13 years. This facet of my teaching life has been most rewarding, in addition to my four decades of teaching at MIT. Of course, during all my teaching years I have practiced architecture, both in this country and in many nations worldwide.

In the final section of the book are some personal thoughts about the future of our work as architects.

The book is my quest for a better way for architects to help the world we live in. If you find all of this too much to read, of course I understand, and if you wish to email me with your thoughts and ideas, please use the email above.

COMMENT

Robert M. MacLeod, AIA
Professor
School of Architecture & Community Design
University of South Florida
Rome, June 2024

In the summer of 2009, shortly after accepting the position as Director of the University of South Florida (USF) School of Architecture & Community Design (SACD), I received a call from College of the Arts Associate Dean and Acting SACD Director, Barton Lee. He recently met a person interested in teaching at the School of Architecture. This individual lived part of the year in nearby St. Petersburg and had a connection to MIT. His name was Jan Wampler.

I knew of Jan Wampler long before he knew of me. I started my graduate studies in the fall of 1984. My good friend and undergraduate classmate from the University of Florida, Andrew Weaver, was studying at MIT. I was up the street at the Harvard GSD. We frequently met to discuss our respective programs, faculty, projects and so forth. Andrew and his colleagues agreed on one thing: Jan Wampler was best faculty member at MIT. He was the person students most wanted to work with in design studio. He offered a unique insight into the discipline of architecture. He was an environmentalist, urbanist, and social engineer; part philosopher; part sage. The uniqueness of place and culture was not lost on him, and he thoughtfully imparted this complex web of wisdom to his students. He was, one might say, a legend.

Born in the emerging shadow of World War Two, Jan came of age as a student and later as an educator at a time when the world of architecture began to acknowledge the sea change of environmentalism, social awareness and gender equality. The academy and the profession were in a compatible quandary. Embracing the moment, Jan – and those of his generation – were simultaneously shaped by the emerging ethos and harnessed the energy of that ethos to reshape the world around them through education and practice.

It is Jan's fearless optimism and belief in the architect's role as a civic leader despite the ongoing backdrop of cynicism, social unrest, consumption, and the recent commonplace inversion of truth, that, in the end, gives greater depth and meaning to his words and deeds.

There is a timelessness to Jan's message: his infectious positivity; his call for the dutiful stewardship of the planet; his insistence that young architects design for people, not programs; and his call to resist the black hole of architectural practice as a tool for developers and banks.

I have seen several Jan Wampler lectures and presentations over the years. Two things are constant as he concludes his talks with a pair of images. One is the Hengshan Hanging Temple in China's Shanxi Province, clinging precariously to a cliffside one hundred feet in the air. This is a gravity defying architecture beyond and, as Bernard Rudofsky might say, without architects. The second image is of four children running, jumping, and laughing with the joyousness and innocence that only children possess. Jan reminds us that these are our clients; this is for whom we design and build.

He further reminds us the bridge between the temple and the joyful children is the role of play, invention, imagination and the fundamental delight of making architecture.

Arriving in the spring of 2011, Jan's impact upon the SACD was quick and profound. His ideas, philosophy and lessons resonated in the thirteen graduate studios taught between 2011 and 2023. He traveled with students to Cuba, Quito, Thailand, Cyprus, and Puerto Rico, among other locales. Students speak of these studios with great fondness and as a defining experience in their education. Many see it as a rite of passage – one they look back upon as shaping their understanding of the role of architecture and architects in society. Their careers have responded to opportunities afforded by Jan's guidance.

The SACD faculty have often called Jan our "junior faculty", given his boundless enthusiasm and energy for teaching and for all things architecture. This translates to Jan's teaching as a similar palpable energy fills his studios. His students frequently work together on group projects, again, affording lessons in life and architecture: collective vision, negotiation, compromise, teamwork. And they are always in the studio.

Jan has been called the Walt Whitman of Architecture and this is an apt moniker. From the Chicago based Poetry Foundation website: *Walt Whitman is America's world poet—a latter-day successor to Homer, Virgil, Dante, and Shakespeare. In Leaves of Grass (1855, 1891-2), he celebrated democracy, nature, love, and friendship. This monumental work chanted praises to the body as well as to the soul...*

In referencing Whitman, one also recalls the intellectual lineage of Ralph Waldo Emerson and Henry David Thoreau. Distinctively American in their collective explorations of a young nation, all idealists, philosophers, poets and educators. All point to Jan, for he is the logical successor to an intellectual exploration borne of abolitionists, naturalists, and transcendentalists.

In recalling Jan's philosophical forebears, it must be noted that he is, in many ways, an urban creature. Having spent most of his professional life in Boston, and more recently on Block Island and in the Tampa Bay area, his affinity for urban life presents itself in his teaching. At SACD he exclusively taught urban design studios. Students learn quickly about "the space between", Jan's shorthand for the life that must exist betwixt and between architecture: the lively and spontaneous activities of street and square. In Wampler World, the space of the street comes before buildings just as the people come before architecture.

In the spring of 2019, Jan composed the Oath for Architects. Moved by the Physicians' Hippocratic Oath, Jan's oath is a pledge to the architecture profession, the environment, and humankind. The oath is administered to every SACD graduating class. It is a promise that reminds us of why we make architecture, why we teach architecture and why we love architecture. It also reminds us of the awesome responsibility and opportunity we have as architects. It is a message from Jan to all students, architects and educators. One I repeat each year with students for their edification. And mine.

On my honor, I hereby take this oath of commitment to the following principles: To maintain the highest ethical and moral standards in my life and my architectural practice; To commit my practice for the good of our planet and humanity; To practice architecture according to its basic aim to provide human shelter and enriched quality of life for all humanity; To treat clients, allied professionals inside and outside of my industry, and the general public with respect, honesty, and integrity; To respect diverse socioeconomic identities, gender issues and rights, and to not discriminate by race, color, religion, sex, age, national origin, sexual orientation, gender identity, disability, and any other basis prohibited by law; To strive to be an enlightened, passionate steward of both the built and the natural environments, address climate change, and conservation of Earth's natural resources; To pass on to the next generation our responsibility to do good for the world through universal, sustainable design that meets the needs of all humankind and protects the Earth; By taking this oath, I have accepted my duty toward the betterment of civilization, its buildings, communities, and ecosystems.

INTERVIEW

Jan Wampler
June 19, 2024

The following interview was conducted by Paul Lukez over a period of several months, in four parts. Each part was several hours long and was recorded in Paul's office or over Zoom. The four parts totaled about 100 pages of text.

Paul has taught architecture for over 20 years. He was a full-time professor at MIT for seven years. He has also taught at Washington University, RISD, Roger Williams University, and Tsinghua University.

He is a graduate of Miami University (BED) and MIT (M'Arch), where he received the Henry Adams Award and Goody Prize. He also wrote a book, *Suburban Transformations* (Princeton Architectural Press, October 2007), which proposes strategies and processes for transforming suburbs into more sustainable environments.

Paul began as a student in my studio at MIT. Then he became my teaching assistant and worked in my office. Now he owns and operates a very successful architectural practice. But most important, Paul is a dear friend to me.

The parts of the interview have now been edited and combined as one text, and they now amount to about 50 pages of text. I had intended them to cover most of my life, beginning when I was about six years old up to the present time, when I am almost 85. Most of Paul's interviews concerned my relationship with the profession of architecture, even though there are personal experiences in the process of design.

The interview is now in eight parts, and each part is followed by architectural work related to the text, as well as words that I call "Soul Songs." This is not poetry, as I am not a poet; I am simply noting my experience along my journey. The interview ends with a display of my present work and my thoughts about the future of my profession and how I believe the world should be in the future.

The interview has been extensively edited by several editors, including Todd Larson, my constant editor over the years, and Elizabeth Reed, who is both a critic of my writing and an excellent editor. I have discovered that writing and a conversation are nowhere the same. In a conversation I tend to ramble, where in text I am much more logical, especially when it is in edited form. Nevertheless, they both tell my story.

I also incorporated a story within the story into the interview, which is perhaps much more important to the understanding of a person. What I have learned from this experience is that the story within is very simple. What holds the story together is the love one has for oneself and for others.

Without this, there is no real story. Please read with that in mind. Thank you.

PART 1

Paul: Jan, maybe you can talk about your early life and how you ended up at RISD. But before we do that, I wanted to share with you some questions. Architecture critic Robert Campbell referred to you as "the Walt Whitman of architecture." Why did he associate you with Whitman? Besides the fact that you and Walt had similar-shaped beards.

Jan: I think he made that connection in response to an exhibition of my work at MIT which included what I called my "words"— not exactly poetry — but words that express a connection with nature. And there was a lot that related to the Common Man and Woman, a central theme for Whitman. Also, Bob Campbell may have reviewed my first book, *All Their Own* or heard Susan Stamberg's interview about it on NPR. The book is about my travels across the U.S. to find non-architects, ordinary people who built their own unconventional homes. I think he put all that together and called me "the Walt Whitman of Architects." I've never asked him why, but it became a label for me.

Paul: And one that you carried proudly.

Jan: Yes, of course, Walt Whitman was my hero. When I was a kid, I read *Leaves of Grass* and was so taken by it.

Paul: What interested you in *Leaves of Grass*? Do you see similarities in the way Whitman works and your approach to architecture and poetry?

Jan: I think Whitman's experience in the Civil War — he was an ambulance driver and nurse — was both enlightening and devastating for him, as my experience traveling around the world, seeing how people lived, inspired me but was also devastating. I think that influenced Whitman's life and work. He was very young when he was doing his ambulance job, about the age I was when I was traveling.

I think Bob made the connection from — I use the word loosely — poetry, poetic pieces I wrote in which he saw something that related to Whitman's poetry. For me the affinity with Whitman was early experiences which strongly influenced our development and our work. For example, my values were shaped by my family of origin, socioeconomic background and experiences seeing people in slums of Latin America where I traveled.

That leads to something else. I grew up on a farm in Ohio.

Paul: Right. You're from Ohio, too?

Jan: That's right. I was born there. My maternal grandparents had a very poor farm. Whitman's family were farm people without much formal education and Whitman himself was largely self-taught. His father struggled to support the family by farming among other things. My grandfather had no formal education; my grandmother left school when she was twelve and joined a circus. I loved the farm. Being there had a lot to do with my desire to be an architect, in two ways. First, the barn was my domain. I spent a lot of time there building huts and other structures and taking care of my grandfather's five horses.

Secondly, from a traveling salesman who came up the lane one day my grandmother bought me *The Book of Knowledge*, which was like an encyclopedia. It cost 49 cents or 99 cents per monthly volume. I loved those books and studied them intently. I remember the first time I saw pictures of cathedrals with light coming through the stained-glass windows and comparing those images with the barn where light filtered through knotholes in the boards. That made a lasting impression.

Paul: So, you're talking about the importance of your youth and how it shaped your life.

Jan: Yes. I greatly respected my grandparents who had no formal education, no money, but a deep intuitive appreciation for things, particularly nature, hard work and living off the land. When I was seven, eight and nine, I spent a lot of time with my grandfather in the fields, helping as much as I could and looking at things in nature. Once we stopped to watch a tumblebug make a nest. The bug rolled pieces of dung into balls and used them to make its house. We must have spent an hour that way when my grandfather should have been working in the fields. I think times like that have come out in my architecture.

My paternal grandparents I barely knew. I met my paternal grandmother just once. From what I know she was an amazing woman who had been a very active suffragette protesting for women's right to vote. This did not happen until 1920. My grandfather was in World War I, which may explain why he was a pacifist. He was also part of an Ohio group of Prairie Radicals who believed that small farms would be bought out by large corporations. The two of them had lunch at the County Court House and protested these issues regularly.

My one meeting with my grandmother took place in her house which was piled high with books and magazines, making it hard for me to find a place to sit and talk. Midway through a sentence, dressed in a black suit with white gloves, she wheeled out her bicycle — she was in her late 80s or early 90s — and said she had to go give her speech at the Court House and would be right back. When she returned 25 minutes later, she picked up the sentence right where she'd left off. I was impressed! Later I realized I did know her: She was the woman who would give us neighborhood kids peanut-butter cookies and milk on our way home from school. We always hoped she would be there. I can still smell those cookies ...

Because of complicated family dynamics I did not know who she was, but she must have known that I was her grandson. What wonderful grandparents I never knew!

My mother was a very resourceful, creative woman. She wanted to go to New York City and be a clothes designer but there was no money for that, and women did not engage in such ventures at that time. Instead, she designed and sewed clothes for neighbors, laundered, made candies and rented out rooms in our house, including mine. That was why I went to my grandparents' farm where there was food and room for me.

Due to the early disintegration of my parents' marriage, I didn't meet my father until I was in my 30's. That life-changing event came about accidentally. At the time I was Chief Architect for the Boston 76 World's Fair. The Associated Press did an interview with me that was published in papers around the country. A cousin whom I did not know lived in Salt Lake City, read it, called and asked what I knew about my father. I told him "Nothing. I don't even know if he is alive."

Motivated by his religion's tenet that family bonds should never be broken, this cousin gave me my father's phone number and location. I carried that information in my pocket for weeks before I found the courage to use it. I called and said, "I think I am your son." He replied, "I think I am your father." We joked later that we were almost speechless then but later we talked for hours every night and caught up on our lives.

One night I told him I had worked in Puerto Rico. He said he had too, in a small town on the west side. It turned out to be the same town where I'd worked. He asked where I stayed and I replied, "At the old hotel on the plaza in the room on the second floor, overlooking the plaza and church." He said that was the room where he'd stayed 30 years earlier! Later when I visited his home it was like seeing a decades-older version of myself: same gestures, body language, demeanor. Meeting him so late in life was remarkable. Maybe there's an advantage to meeting your parents as an adult without the emotional baggage of the growing pains of childhood!

Paul: That is a fascinating story about your father. Your grandfather and grandmother lived in nature. And, as such, they were more dependent on nature. Consequently, they perhaps had a heightened awareness of nature and all its forces, in ways that people who are living in urban environments cannot comprehend.

Jan: That is true. They passed on that awareness to me. In Ohio, you could look out over the flat landscape which seemed to go on forever. Charles Dickens visited Ohio in the 1840s. At one time Ohio was completely forested, but when Dickens was there, they were burning tree stumps to make fields for growing food. He asked — not his exact words — "What will become of a country that has no regard for nature?"

Paul: No, I didn't know that.

Jan: As you know white settlers moved West across the country, claiming land as they went. Now, when you drive from Cleveland to Columbus or points east, it's all farm fields. When I lived on the farm we would sit on the porch, watching a storm approach and my grandfather would tell me where it was and where it was going. He'd say, "It's over Columbus, don't miss it." In 1864, 160 acres of federal land were given to anyone who would live there, farm it and grow one tree. This explains the very large tree on our land. I remember many lessons of this kind from my childhood. They intrigued me and made me want to learn more about the world.

Paul: You didn't have Instagram; you were free of social media distractions. This must have allowed you to focus on nature, the sky, storms, and other spectacles that nature provided. There must have been plenty of sources for amusement and education.

Jan: Yes, all those things interested and stimulated me. Also, formative was *The Book of Knowledge* which I mentioned earlier and still have. I can open to almost any page and tell you what will be on the next one. I learned to read and write from those volumes. They were powerful tools which I studied intently. I still remember all kinds of things gleaned from them. I wonder if kids today will have the same experience with the Internet. There's no question that they have access to much more information than we had but with a different way of accessing it. With an encyclopedia or book, you had to make conscious decisions about what you were looking at. And when you opened to a page, especially in an encyclopedia, it was like being in a candy shop with so many exciting options to choose from. You didn't know what you would come across and where it might lead. That may be like the Internet.

Paul: Yes, maybe due to the degree of randomness in the search process, at least in earlier versions of the Internet.

Jan: I compare it to a library card catalog. You went in to search for a book, rifled through the card catalog and found a dog-eared card covered with fingerprints. "I wonder what that book is?" When you went into the stacks looking for your book, you would see others beside it and start reading them.

Paul: But the Internet is not quite the same. Now algorithms are written to align with your past preferences and interests, limiting the more random links one might encounter in a library stack. The opportunity for those more random and unexpected discoveries found in the card catalog or library shelves are rich. So, yes – you were lucky to have that exposure to your encyclopedias and *Book of Knowledge*.

Jan: Oh, my God. It was a world of ideas, and wonderful for me!

Paul: What do you think your grandparents would think of you if they were alive, seeing the incredible range of experiences you've had and all that you've accomplished, despite growing up in modest circumstances?

Jan: I think they would be very proud. My grandmother was proud of everything I did. My grandfather too. I used to build little houses with him. If someone visited, they knew they had to bring boxes for me. My prizes were Quaker Oats Cereal round containers I'd cut up and make into weird forms. But there were some things I couldn't do for myself. While I slept by the stove — the farm's only source of heat, and we had no electricity or water — my grandfather after a long day in the field, would be up late cutting out pieces of cardboard. The next morning, I would find the pieces he'd cut to use in my housebuilding, like Christmas every day. I believe he'd be proud of where this has led.

I want to say more about my grandmother. As I said, she was in the circus as a fortune teller. Later people would come to the farm to hear her predictions. This provided a little cash income. I used to hide behind the couch and listen. She had a good track record.

The last time I saw her she told me she would die in a week, and she did. She took both my hands, sat me down next to her and said to listen carefully. I loved her deeply but thought she was a little kooky. She said I would be confronted with death three times and if I reached into my inner self for strength, after the third time I would live to be a wise old man. Well, I have had my three encounters with death. I did as she told me, and I am certainly getting old, but I am not sure about the wise part.

My grandparents never went to school and most of my family never finished school. As far as I know I am the only one in my family who went to college.

Paul: Why do you think that is? Were you the exception?

Jan: Very much the exception. I've thought a lot about how that happened. I don't know the answer. Family patterns carried over from one generation to the next, more in the past than now. I don't know a lot about my grandfather's past except that he was in a horse act in the circus. He told the story that he was one of several children in the horse act. One day he took two horses from the tent to water them and during that time the circus burned down, killing his parents and siblings while they tried to save the other horses. Circuses often burned to the ground since they had a canvas tent and open flame lamps for light. Alone in the world, my grandfather rode the two remaining horses to Colorado to find his uncle and joined another circus where he met my grandmother.

Besides nature, another big ingredient of my childhood was the railroad that went through the land behind the farm. Every night I would go down and sit on a bank close to the tracks. I kept track of each train, how many cars were on it, whether it was on time or late, etc., I was up high enough to look down into the dining cars of passenger trains as they went by and see what people were eating. I often wondered where they were heading and what their lives were like, so different from mine and my family's.

Paul: What did that mean to you?

Jan: I think that reflected my drive to know more. I've always had a strong sense of curiosity, of wanting to explore. I think it was rooted in these early experiences.

Paul: So, seeing the trains go by your farm allowed you to imagine where these people were going, what they were eating and what kinds of different experiences they might be exposed to when they reached their destinations. Were those trains connecting you to a larger world beyond Marion, Ohio?

Jan: It is true that the trains connected me to the wider world. But the railroad did something else which fascinated me. At that time, in the '40s, a lot of people who were called "hobos" rode the rails. I saw them as bright, witty, and adventurous. They would get off the train and go to houses looking for a meal. My grandmother had a tradition of setting an extra plate at the table in case someone knocked on our door, so they wouldn't feel embarrassed to come in and eat. She was very generous, and always let them in. I would stare at them the whole time, listening to their stories and wondering where they were going. I had a lot going for me in terms of leaving that farm, otherwise I could still be there.

Paul: Do you really think so, though?

Jan: I think it would be a little like being a caged animal. I had a lot of luck, including free train passes because my stepfather worked for the railroad. I was able to travel around the country. The railroad ran from Chicago to New York so those were my two big destinations where I went often. I have no idea why anyone let me do that when I was so young.

Paul: How old were you at the time?

Jan: I was in 6th, 7th or 8th grade, which would make me between 11 and 13.

Paul: You were granted much freedom at such a young age.

Jan: I was, and that experience of going to New York, Chicago, and other cities for the first time was incredibly exciting. I imagine it blew me away. I guess I was always interested in seeing what was going on around the corner, on the next block and beyond.

Paul: So, there's a sort of fearlessness to your endeavors and adventures, as a youth but also in your professional life. You have been able and willing to put yourself into new environments which are deeply challenging and not at all familiar. In the process you propelled yourself into a whole other domain of experiences and opportunities.

Jan: I've thought about this a lot, too. I've done some foolish, risky things, and I was so naïve and innocent. But I was lucky. I did nothing bad and nothing terrible happened. Those experiences helped formulate how I thought about things. Especially seeing what other peoples' lives were like. When I went to the slums in La Perla, Puerto Rico, I said, "I want to go see and meet the people who live there." The people in charge said, "We will send a police escort down with you, because it's very dangerous." And I said, "No, I don't want that." A police escort would have been the kiss of death. So, I went down there alone, outside the wall of the old city, slowly moving into the slum area. I was in danger, but it didn't occur to me that something bad might happen. The fearlessness came and may still come from not fully recognizing the level of danger.

Paul: But on the other hand, just being so excited and curious about the world allowed you to momentarily forget the true danger you placed yourself in. Do you think this could also be an unconscious response, this fearlessness you had? Were there times in your life where you were confronting that fear and decided you were just going to face it head-on?

Jan: When I was 12, 13, 14, in those days the thing to do with the family on Sundays was to take a ride in the car. This was a big deal because cars represented freedom. When we stopped somewhere, the story goes, I was out the door instantly and gone, exploring to the point where the local police had to be called in to locate me. I was always that way, wanting to know what was around the corner. I get impatient with my students when we travel somewhere and end up in a new old town, and they walk down the street looking at their iPhones, talking. I say, "Hey man, look around!" Because I was always so excited by the opportunity to experience and explore new and different places. My curiosity got me into situations which were a little tricky, but somehow, I managed them well enough and gained so much from them. The new technologies create a mediated "reality" in place of the kind of direct experience that I believe is more dynamic, impactful, and conducive to learning.

Maternal grandparents; I strongly suggest having your grandparents raise you rather than your parents…both my grandparents were great mentors to me for my future life. c. 1958.

Paternal grandparents. Both were very active in political issues, grandmother with women's rights and grandfather with farmers' rights.

Mother. She was a very enterprising woman able to take care of herself. Age unknown.

Father. I met him when I was about 35, a wonderful man, writer, active in Native American rights. Circa 1980

Memory 1

I want to walk on the alley again
With my grandfather on a cool
summer night
Asking about the stars in
the alley
As a small one might

Hearing it is only small pieces
of glass
Reflecting the light of the moon

What joy, what love, a moment
of discover

Memory 2

We stopped in the field'
To watch a tumble bug
Rolling dung to make a nest
Like a house

We stayed for long time
When my grandfather
Should have been in the fields

What joy, what love a moment
of discover

Innocense

i lie on the beach
and watch as three women
in black and white
walk along the water edge
watching for life from the sea
they stop to explore their
find of a stranded sea urchin
still alive
and
with sticks
they poke and beat the lost
body
till dead

and walk on
their crucifixes
dancing in the sun

Barn that was my central building growing up. Took care of animals and built model towns from boxes. My domain.

Farmyard with horses that I took care of.

PART 2

Paul: So, as we switch topics a bit, let's look toward what your past experiences meant for teaching your students. Given that students today are presented with different challenges and opportunities, and very different ways of seeing the world, how do you guide your students to think about design, societal and environmental issues in a way that creates a better architecture, and a better experience for people?

Jan: Well, that's an interesting question, because I'm just now putting together my assignments for next semester's project in Ukraine. I must tell my students that we can't go to Ukraine. That's impossible; it's dangerous now. But, to design for them, them, we must know Ukraine and the site and people, as well as we know own back yards and neighbors. And we must figure out how to do that.

So, from the start, in the first week I have several assignments of observations from afar. Of course, the Internet makes it possible to get a lot of information, which is good. You can't smell or feel the place, but you can get more objective information than what we used to be able to get. I tell students that information is useless unless you have a point of view about it. I say, "When you present, I don't want to hear just the facts. I want to hear what it feels like, what it means to you, where you can go from there." In the Ukraine situation, this is crucial.

One of the ways I use I call "fresh eyes." By "fresh" I mean they're not directly experiencing it. They're looking at this situation, trying to inform themselves of what it is in emotional, layered ways. Recently I learned that in the Tampa area, the Ukrainians have a church. One of the students' first assignments is to go to that church this Sunday.

Also, I have a student who is organizing a group from that church to be among our clients. They will come into the studio often. I will tell my students that when the church members come, "I want each of you to have at least three questions to ask which are not purely factual, but which get to the heart of what Ukraine feels like."

Paul: There's person-to-person contact, or some direct relationship between the client group, users, and students and designers. Your architecture, your design, your teaching is all about people, right? And so, to operate in these digitally mediated environments is completely counter to the things you believe in. Do you find this to be an ongoing struggle that you consciously are trying to overcome? Or have you just accepted it? Or is it something else?

Jan: No, I haven't accepted it. I do see it as an ongoing struggle and am constantly finding ways to hear and understand what people are thinking. An exercise I use with clients at the start of designing is to ask for three things: I say, "I want you to prepare an outline of all the things you must have in this house." Secondly "I want you to prepare a scrapbook of things you would like to have." My third request is for a scrapbook of things they don't think they could ever have but would like to have. So, I'm trying to get into people's ideas and dreams.

I've been able to approach design in a way that differs from how our profession often operates, in part because I've had the luxury of a steady income from teaching. One benefit of my long MIT career is that it freed me from some of the demands and protocol of relying on architectural commissions.

When I was a student at RISD I would go to the site with my girlfriend, a bottle of wine and something to eat, and stay there overnight. I have continued to do that throughout my career. My point has been to try to feel the site, to experience it intimately. It is important to me to feel the nature of a site, and to hear the needs and dreams of its users, its residents. Those things converge to start a design. I've always done this. I guess I will always and maybe I have the time and luxury of being able to. Whereas, when you're running an office, you've got many deadlines, and it's more challenging. If you're doing a large project in Boston, each time you want to visit the site, even though it's right here you must make a reservation in advance, get it all cleared by the developer, and have escorts. You can't visit the site each time you have a question or need to see a field condition.

It would be great if architects could engage deeply and directly with the people (clients, residents, users) and places (sites, projects) without so many obstacles. This speaks again to creating architecture that's real, tactile, of the earth, about people, about how landscape, architecture and communities come together. I want students to engage in all those aspects, so they learn to design joyful livable places.

Paul: I think there are implications about the way you practice for the future of architecture and how it dovetails with what's going on in the world at large. You don't have a traditional practice, but you have a practice that's very active all around the world. And you're doing all these projects in these sites that are in need and demand of architectural services and better ideas. By extension, you can do this through your teaching and studios.

Have you seen this model evolve? What do you see in its future? Is it something you see your students engaging in as they graduate? Or do you see other ways in which this model has found its roots?

Jan: Residually, I guess I have. But your question was about my model of practice and how/whether I see that evolving in today's world; Is it replicable and scalable? I have some other ideas about that, but I would like to think, first, that our profession is evolving into one where we are often leading the charge to address the larger issues of the world.

Why do lawyers, politicians and developers so often call the shots? Architects are the custodians of the physical world. We know a hell of a lot, are passionate, resourceful, and uniquely skilled to address societal and environmental issues. As a profession, architecture has historically been misunderstood and undervalued compared to law and medicine. Too often we are seen as dilettantes or "just artists" who paint a picture for something that gets built by others. Whereas in medicine for example, Doctors Without Borders, and other professional entities are widely known and celebrated for helping others in need.

We have been too insular. It doesn't help that architecture schools often assign the kind of studio projects that reinforce negative stereotypes.

Paul: Similarly, more and more architects have found their way into the political realm, and a range of other fields. If there's one profession well suited to contributing to solving complex problems in an integrated way, it must be architects. It's also interesting how there's a greater focus on direct learning, that is, learning by doing, by using the studio model as a way of teaching, because teaching and learning take on a new, exciting dimension. Kids learn things by doing things. The lessons learned stay with them for the rest of their lives.

Jan: That gets to another point. I did a project called 10,000 Architects, with the goal of teaching people to be more creative. One of the catalysts for this project was an experience I had in Turkey many years ago. I gave a presentation in a little village, and this kid came up to me — he was about 12 years old. He spoke some English and asked if I could teach him how to be an architect. I thought about it and the next day when I saw him, I asked if he had access to a computer.

"Yeah."

"Do you have access to a camera?"

"Yeah."

When I returned to MIT, we started communicating by email about design projects with this back-and-forth over the next year. I would give him small design assignments which he did and sent back. I lost contact with him, but recently learned that he's been accepted to an architectural program in Turkey. It is amazing that from this little village he was awarded a scholarship to study architecture.

One of our jobs as architects is educating people about our field, because if people understand what we do they are more likely to appreciate the value, craft, and impact of architecture. Recently I presented to a group of people about a previous project I did. I went into more detail than planned, because I got the wrong file — one with all the early sketches of the project, as well as the final ones. Members of the audience expressed amazement at how much work I had put into it and all the considerations involved.
The more we can reveal ourselves to the world, the better. Globalization has made that easier to do than in the past. I know you do this also.

Paul: Our office has done a lot of that kind of what we call "giving back" projects. And in the past, we've done chapels, memorials, dormitories, and clinics. It has been very rewarding. We do it by raising money from our clients often to help fund it and through volunteer labor. And then the rest comes from the firm. Certainly, there's a plethora of issues that need to be addressed that architects can contribute to.

Jan: Just doing small projects could be a huge help if we all did them.

Paul: And it would be great to be able to see ways in which these types of initiatives can continue and evolve and grow, perhaps augmented through sponsorship of other institutional support. Have you thought about that? When thinking of all the studios you've sponsored every year, you've must have had to raise money for each one of these studios. Have you thought about approaching some of the big funders?

Jan: I've never done that. When I did the Black Lives Matter ad for *The New York Times*, I approached it naïvely and informally as in "Hey, could you…?" On the other hand, I have made contacts through MIT with people who have generously funded my studio projects over the years. But I've never gone beyond that. As you get older, you start to think about the impact of past decisions. I made a big mistake when I started my practice. It was an individual practice. A partnership did not appeal to me. If I had partnered with someone who was more adept at marketing and fundraising, it would've been better for the office.

Paul: But that's why I think your model is an interesting one. Especially if you could combine it with the new advances in technologies and how people work and collaborate across borders and professional domains. And doing this with Ukraine.

Jan: The first review will be on Zoom so people in Ukraine can participate. However, for the final review I'm trying to find ways to get them to come here. And I'm in touch with a consortium of architects, planners and others from Ukraine who are working together on temporary housing. I asked them to send photos of themselves that I can show the students tomorrow. I figured I might get half a dozen: I got close to 80! They're still thinking in the Soviet mode of design: austere, hulking, utilitarian. Even the younger generation. They are incredibly expressive in a poetic way. But they're very pragmatic when it comes to architecture. They have said very clearly that they're looking for new ideas, fresh ideas.

Ukraine Studio Project

Work by:
Phyo Hay Mar Kyaw (Sophia), Layan Alkaelani,
Mariam Aldelamy

The Urban Architecture Studio significantly enhanced our skills as designers by encouraging us to adopt a comprehensive and energy efficient approach. Through the Ukrainian village project, we learned the critical importance of integrating environmental context into our designs. We developed agricultural, water, and electrical systems that were not only functional but also in harmony with nature. This class emphasized the need for innovation and sustainable solutions, deepening our understanding of how architecture can positively impact communities. The collaborative environment and focus on real-world problem-solving equipped us with the ability to become more thoughtful, resourceful, and empathetic designers.

We are now equipped to address complex urban challenges with a sustainable and community-focused approach, drawing on the invaluable experiences and skills gained from the Urban Architecture Studio. This course has refined our design abilities and instilled a deep commitment to creating architecture that truly benefits and enhances communities.

Our growth and success in this course are greatly attributable to Professor Jan Wampler, who continuously challenged us within a supportive group environment. His guidance pushed us to explore new ideas and approaches, fostering a deeper appreciation for the complexities of sustainable design and community impact. Professor Wampler reminded us of the fundamental role of architecture in serving people, urging us to maintain a constant focus on designing with their needs and experiences in mind.

"The Earth is what we all have in common."
- Wendell Berry

64′
128′
256′
512′
CALE: 1″=64′

"Why" Statement

Following our initial discussions, we brainstormed key elements necessary for our town. Due to Ukraine's water pollution, we wanted to develop a water system that will serve the economy, as well as having agricultural units envisioned as "walk-through greenhouses," providing a unique experience and versatile functionality in different weather conditions. These factors form the independence and identity of the town, enabling it to support itself and the surrounding cities. Our village aspires to empower and inspire the Ukrainian people, providing them with hope and a renewed sense of purpose.

Draft Model

The Ukrainian site location sits just north of a river, so utilizing our surrounding context became our initial step. By creating agricultural, water and electrical sustainability we suggest an overall design that will utilize nature as best as we can.

A water purification system will be utilized for production of drinking water for the residents and distribution to nearby cities. This water plant is located just above the river line. Agricultural units are placed on the east cliff, and will be used for produce by the residents of the community. Greenhouses will also be used for agricultural purposes. Aerial views of the model show how the neighborhoods branch off from the central spine and create residential areas that are more private and quiet. Focusing on creating tight knit spaces in the areas closest to the plaza, eventually the residential units iceberg out into denser vegetation and into the landscape. The major industrial product will be water, and water functions will be the core of our town. The water fixtures serve different purposes; three ponds house fish as a food source, and the water channels that stream though all the pedestrian paths serve as monuments.

Paths and Places

The central pathway plan highlights the main pedestrian pathway that travels throughout the neighborhoods. This datum helps connect the village with the surrounding landscape conditions. The key public spaces are highlighted; the main plaza (1), the greenhouses in each neighborhood (2), the water purification plant (3), the parking lot (4), and the memorial (5).

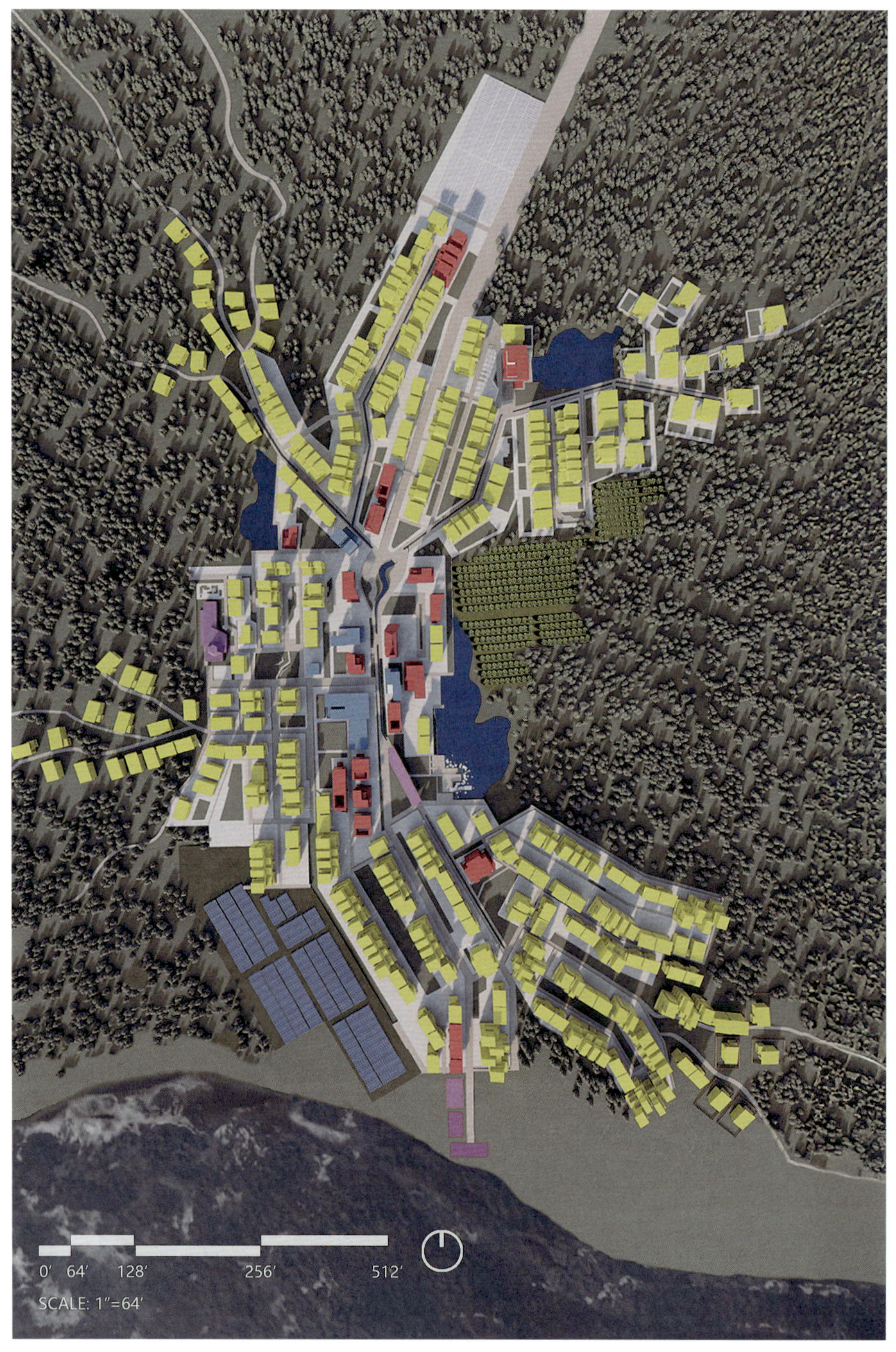

Building Use

The building use plan emphasizes the organization of the village, and the flow of the commercial, institutional, public and residential units. With the yellow representing residential (including 4-row houses, 2-row houses, and single home, red representing commercial, purple highlighting industrial buildings, and blue representing public buildings.

Circulation

The circulation plan illustrates the primary and secondary pathways that connect and surround the village. The yellow represents pedestrian pathways, while the dark orange on the top shows non-pedestrian paths, and the light orange shows the main path through the neighborhood that will be used to transport products with electric golf carts running at specific times, and finally the white circle highlights a 5 minute walking radius. It can be seen that from the central plaza space all neighborhoods are less than a 5 minute distance.

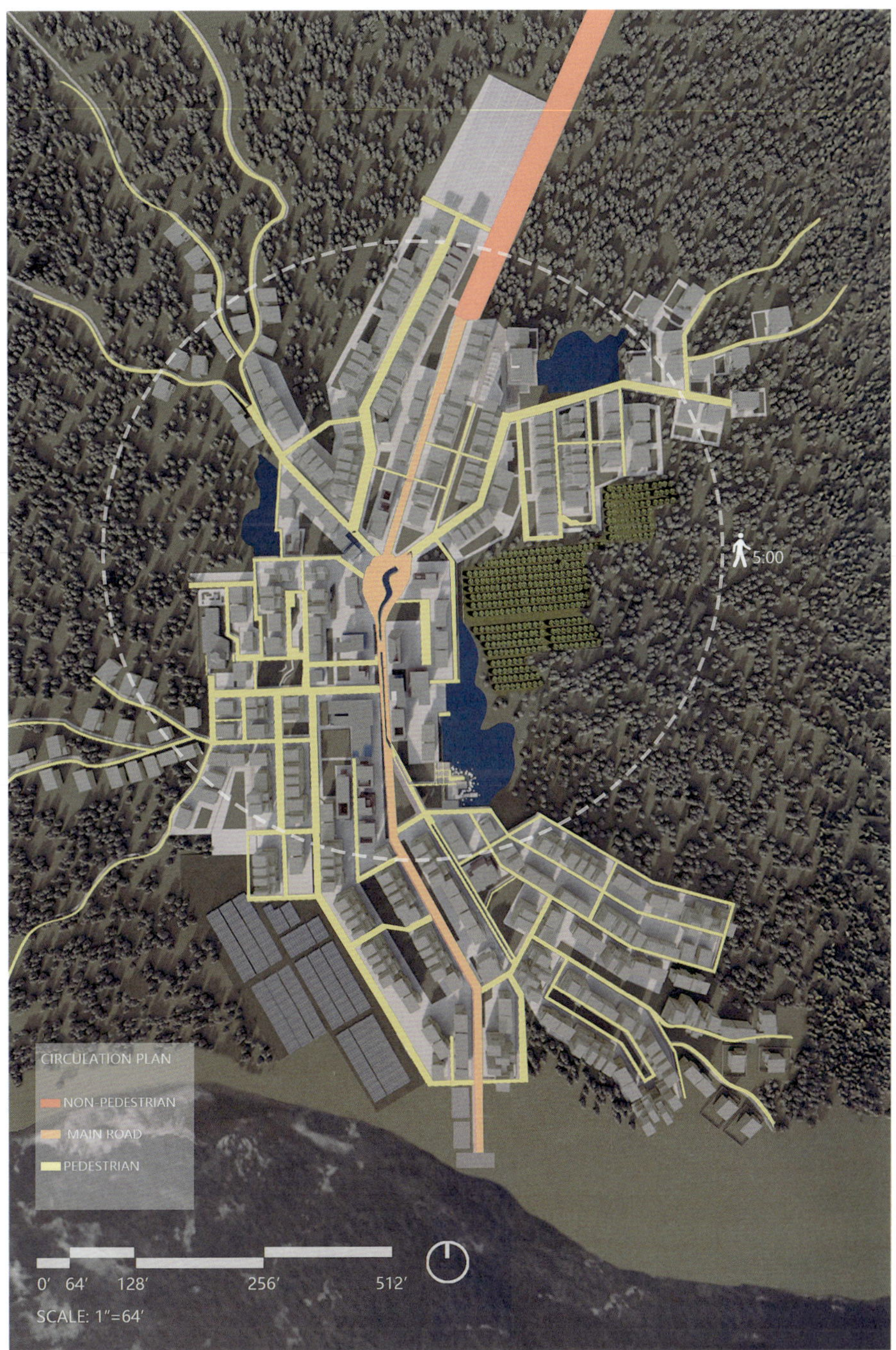

Section Model

Following the neighborhoods, a 3-part section model of the site was developed physically. There is a close focus on the division and connection between public and private space, so the mode depicts the area of the West neighborhood where the public plaza and the residential neighborhoods intersect. Development of the river line that moves through the town was necessary, as it became more interactive and experiential for the residents. As it comes to the central plaza space, the scale of the water becomes larger and more organic.

SLM
NOVOSILKY, UKRAINE

Our Family

Alina and Daniela are recent widows who reside in Novosilky, Ukraine. They both lost their husbands in the ongoing war and have been trying to rebuild their lives since. They've been childhood friends for as long as they can remember and both have kids. Alina has a set of twins and a teenage son, and Daniella also has a set of twins and a teenage daughter as well as another young daughter. After their tragic loss, the women decided it would be best financially and environmentally for them to merge families and have a household where they can support one another. They both have a passion for gardening and cooking.

Single Family Home

In the floor plans developed for the widows, their interests were taken into account, so all of the homes have a restaurant on the first floor, with both interior and outdoor seating. They also have a private greenhouse in their home that sources the products for their restaurant. Moreover, the kitchen is shared for private use as well as their restaurant. The entrance into the single family home is through the east end. The second floor houses bedrooms for all 6 children and the women, as well as a balcony space.

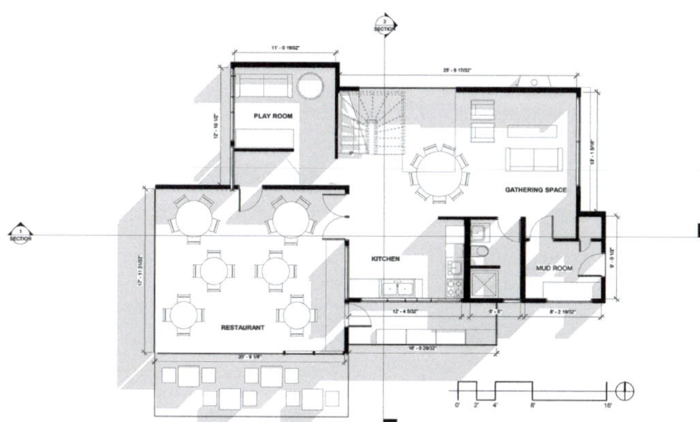

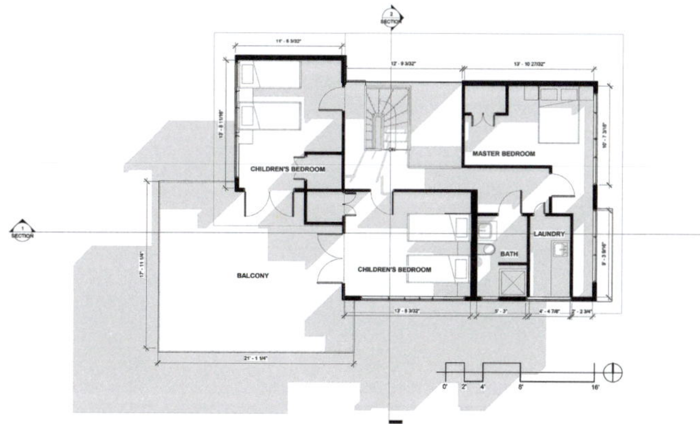

Memorial - The Final Farewell

"The Final Farewell" is a waterfall created through the water path that flows from the ground over a granite walkway. The water channel, which runs throughout the neighborhoods, inscribed with names of those who passed, is the village's homage to the deceased. The monument is the final passage of the water channel, and as the water disperses into the pond, it encapsulates the final farewell to the heroes. The final farewell is always the hardest: the waterfall symbolizes the lives lost, and the rigid stones symbolize those who still stand. The water attempts to pass through as the stones cling onto the ripples, acting as a barrier, desperate to hold on to their lives. But no matter how they fight, the water must still run through. The space has the feeling of a sanctuary. The splashing of the water in the secluded area of the memorial gives visitors background noise that blocks out sounds from outside and allows a moment of peace and contemplation. You might start to feel that you're being swept up in something powerful. Not just observing it but participating in it. Being changed by it.

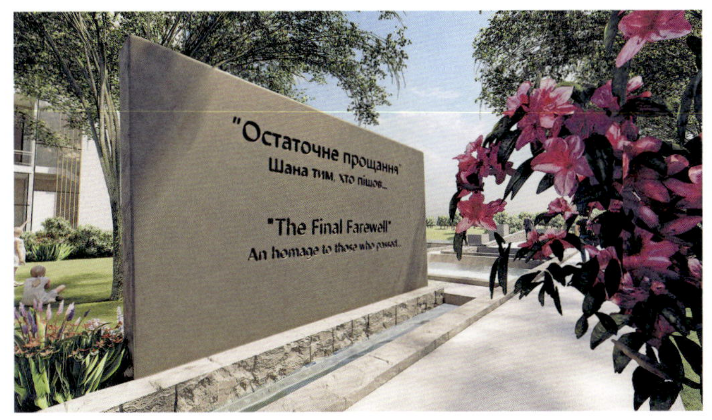

"Остаточне прощання"
Шана тим, хто пішов...
"The Final Farewell"
An homage to those who passed...

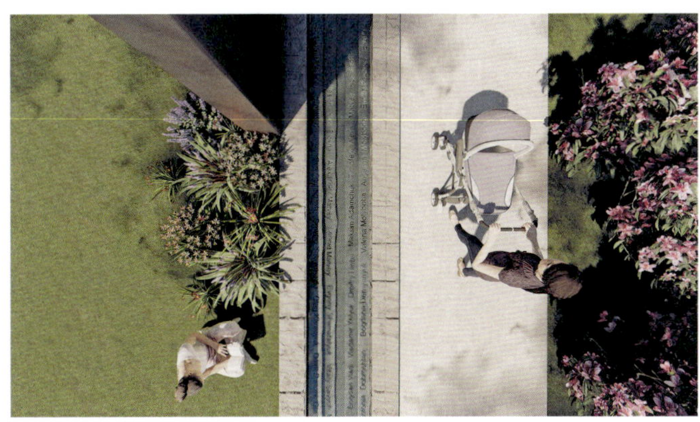

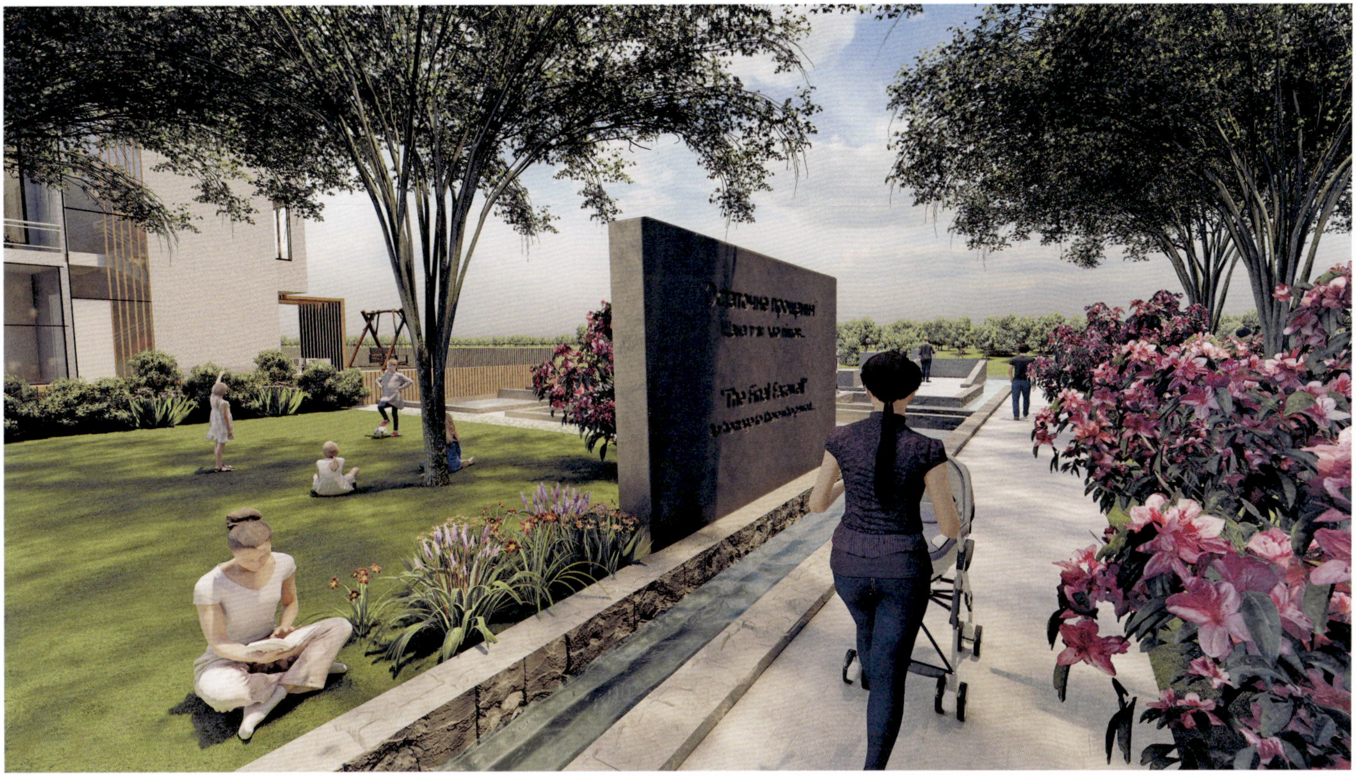
"The Final Farewell"

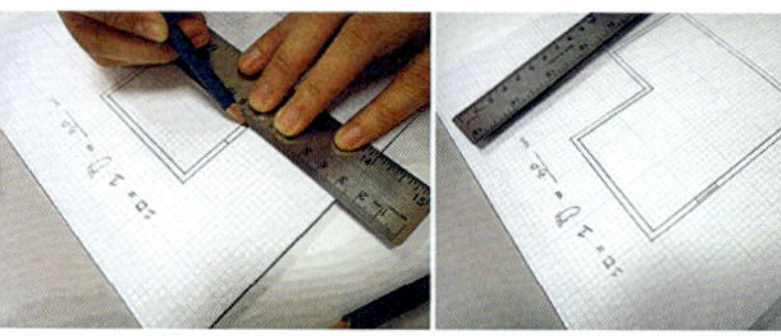

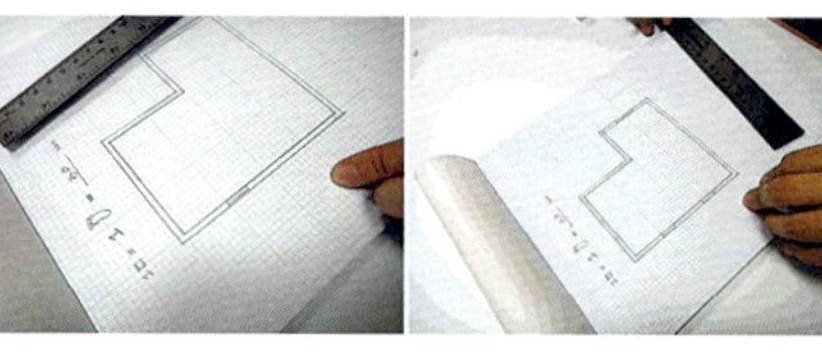

10,000 Architects

10,000 Architects is an online program designed to teach young people the fundamentals of architecture. It is intended for those with little opportunity to attend architecture school due to their location or insufficient funds. This program may help students attend school and receive a scholarship after taking its course.

10,000 Architects is a simple course that teaches people how to think about architecture and start designing. It begins with the process of measurement, using the human body as a scale; the human body's dimensions can be used to determine the sizes of rooms or places in the environment. For example, most human feet are about 12 inches long, a spread-out hand measures about 8 inches, and a typical step on a stair is about 30 inches long. By using these dimensions, we can determine the size of a room or a house.

To begin, count the number of steps you take walking across a room, and then multiply that number by the dimensions of your steps; this will give you the size of the room you are walking in. You can also determine the height of the room by spreading out your hand, counting the number of "hands" totaling the room's height, and multiplying that number by the measurement of your spread-out hand.

Then measure the size of a typical box on a sheet of graph paper, and use the box's dimensions to determine the size of the room. Transfer those dimensions onto the graph paper by drawing a typical house plan with doors and windows. Once the plan is drawn, the next step is to make an architectural model from the plan using cardboard, a small knife, and glue. If cardboard is not available, use material from food containers or leftover boxes. You will also need a hard straight edge for cutting the cardboard, such as a ruler or an architectural triangle. In the beginning, go very slowly so as not to cut your fingers or hand; with practice it will be easier to construct a model of your existing home or a proposal for a new design. (See illustrations of how this is done on the next page.)

Young man who asked me if I could teach him how to be an architect.

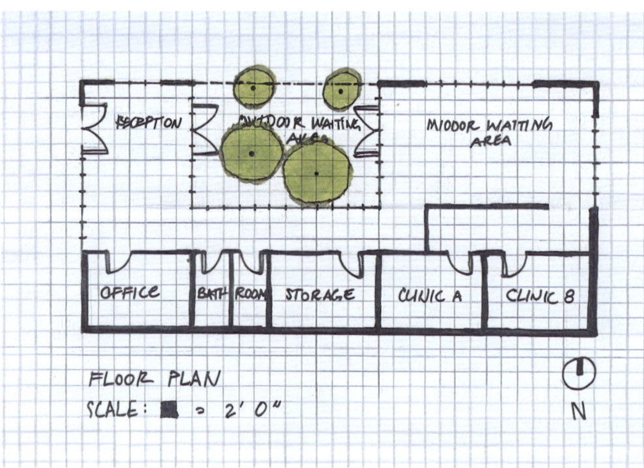
RECEPTION
OUTDOOR WAITING AREA
INDOOR WAITING AREA
OFFICE
BATH ROOM
STORAGE
CLINIC A
CLINIC B
FLOOR PLAN
SCALE: ■ = 2' 0"
N

This house was a place where I lived for the first twelve years of my life, and it is one of the best places for me to live and to visit. It is located in a very small town in Bani, Dominican Republic, called Boca Canasta. This house has two floors, four bedrooms, two bathrooms, a kitchen, two living rooms, and a garage. On the right, I first entered the living room, followed by the kitchen and the second living room. On the left, the first room was my grandmother's bedroom, followed by one bathroom, another bedroom, and finally my bedroom, which is now part of the second living room. On the second floor was the last bedroom and bathroom; this was my mother and father's space. Each of us had our own room and space there. This was why I shared this house with my family and friends most of the time.

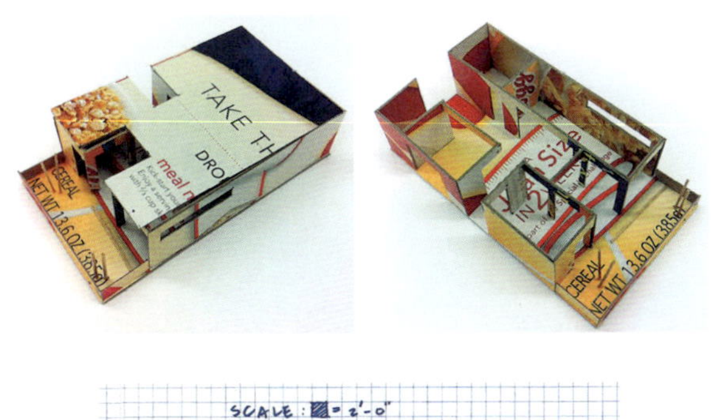

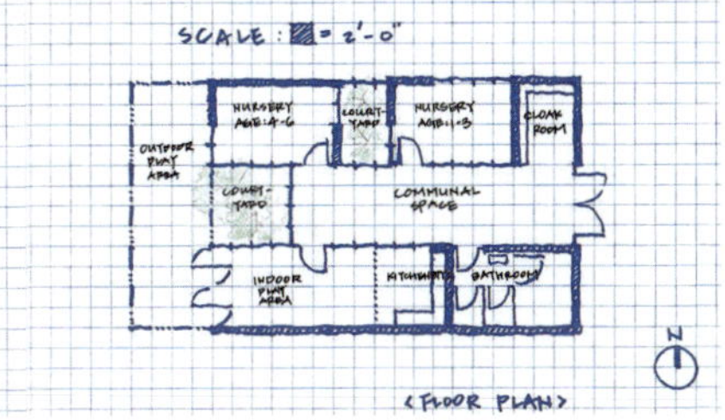

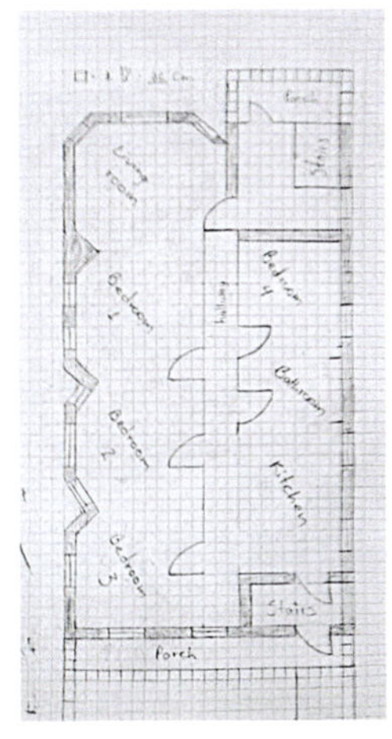

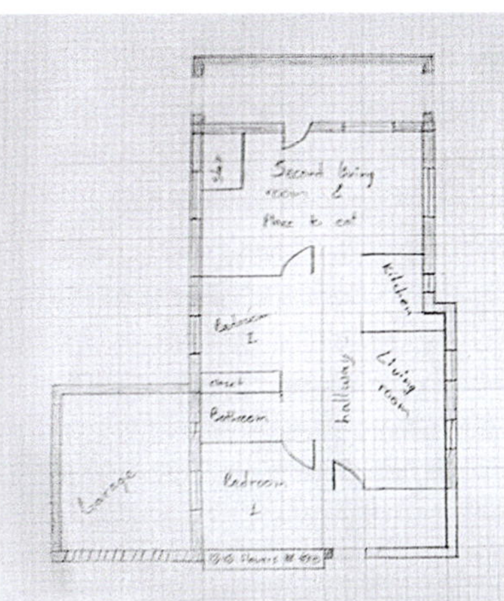

Final project of future architect

Beware of the past
if you travel and view the
    monuments
    of the past
    churches
    pyramids
    palaces
    Roman ruins
        and all other monuments
that we know even cathedrals

please remember this
    these buildings were
    built by many
    often slaves of the ruling
    class,
        the wealthy
        the powerful
        the rulers of religion

they were built by many
but used by only a few

can we really
appreciate
accept
architecture
    that has suppressed
    citizens
    even enslaved them

    beautiful buildings built
    by the exploitations
    of ordinary citizens

I want to feel the wind across my face
On a cold sun filled day
On a hill
Oh what joy
Those days filled with wonder
So many years ago

I want to see the light of the sun
At sunset when the light is golden
Dancing on the floor
Through the house
What a joy to see

I want to hear the trees whisper
Wind moving through the pines
To a dance not known
Near a cold lake
So many years ago

I want to love these delights
Never changing
Always different
What a joy to see

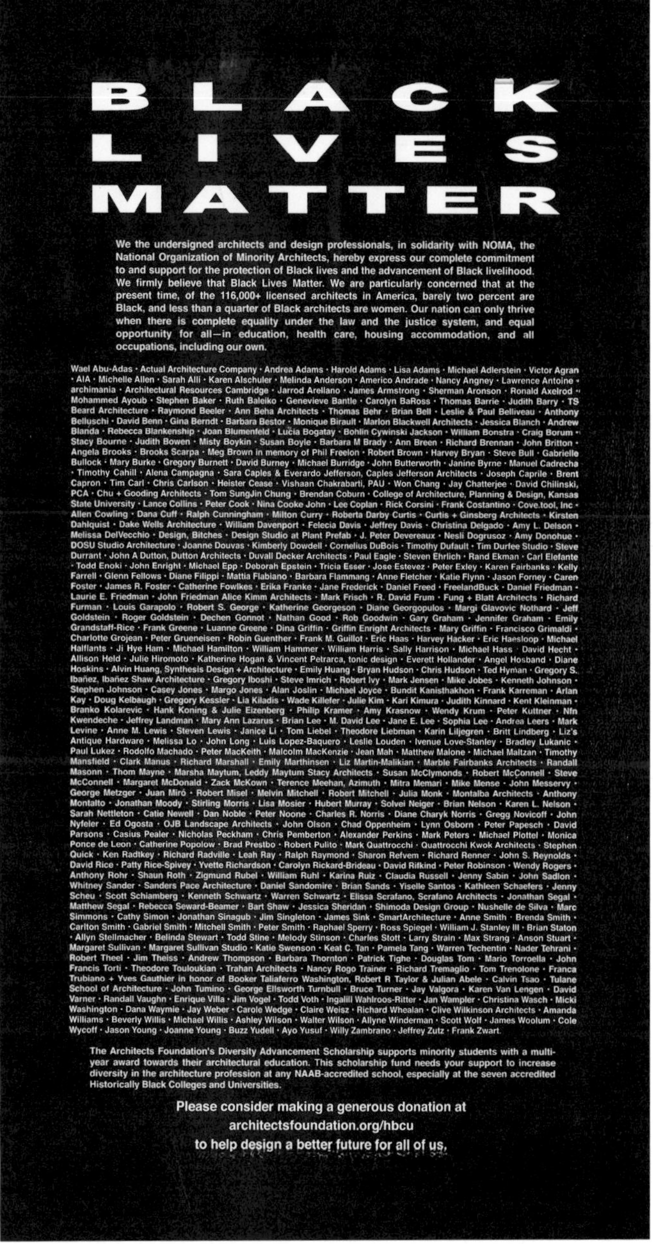

BLACK LIVES MATTER

We the undersigned architects and design professionals, in solidarity with NOMA, the National Organization of Minority Architects, hereby express our complete commitment to and support for the protection of Black lives and the advancement of Black livelihood. We firmly believe that Black Lives Matter. We are particularly concerned that at the present time, of the 116,000+ licensed architects in America, barely two percent are Black, and less than a quarter of Black architects are women. Our nation can only thrive when there is complete equality under the law and the justice system, and equal opportunity for all—in education, health care, housing accommodation, and all occupations, including our own.

Wael Abu-Adas · Actual Architecture Company · Andrea Adams · Harold Adams · Lisa Adams · Michael Adlerstein · Victor Agran · AIA · Michelle Allen · Sarah Alli · Karen Alschuler · Melinda Anderson · Americo Andrade · Nancy Angney · Lawrence Antoine · archimania · Architectural Resources Cambridge · Jarrod Arellano · James Armstrong · Sherman Aronson · Ronald Axelrod · Mohammed Ayoub · Stephen Baker · Ruth Baleiko · Genevieve Bantle · Carolyn BaRoss · Thomas Barrie · Judith Barry · TS Beard Architecture · Raymond Beeler · Ann Beha Architects · Thomas Behr · Brian Bell · Leslie & Paul Belliveau · Anthony Belluschi · David Benn · Gina Berndt · Barbara Bestor · Monique Birault · Marlon Blackwell Architects · Jessica Blanch · Andrew Blanda · Rebecca Blankenship · Joan Blumenfeld · Lucia Bogatay · Bohlin Cywinski Jackson · William Bonstra · Craig Borum · Stacy Bourne · Judith Bowen · Misty Boykin · Susan Boyle · Barbara M Brady · Ann Breen · Richard Brennan · John Britton · Angela Brooks · Brooks Scarpa · Meg Brown in memory of Phil Freelon · Robert Brown · Harvey Bryan · Steve Bull · Gabrielle Bullock · Mary Burke · Gregory Burnett · David Burney · Michael Burridge · John Butterworth · Janine Byrne · Manuel Cadrecha · Timothy Cahill · Alena Campagna · Sara Caples & Everardo Jefferson, Caples Jefferson Architects · Joseph Caprile · Brent Capron · Tim Carl · Chris Carlson · Heister Cease · Vishaan Chakrabarti, PAU · Won Chang · Jay Chatterjee · David Chilinski, PCA · Chu + Gooding Architects · Tom SungJin Chung · Brendan Coburn · College of Architecture, Planning & Design, Kansas State University · Lance Collins · Peter Cook · Nina Cooke John · Lee Coplan · Rick Corsini · Frank Costantino · Cove.tool, Inc · Allen Cowling · Dana Cuff · Ralph Cunningham · Milton Curry · Roberta Darby Curtis · Curtis + Ginsberg Architects · Kirsten Dahlquist · Dake Wells Architecture · William Davenport · Felecia Davis · Jeffrey Davis · Christina Delgado · Amy L. Delson · Melissa DelVecchio · Design, Bitches · Design Studio at Plant Prefab · J. Peter Devereaux · Nesli Dogrusoz · Amy Donohue · DOSU Studio Architecture · Joanne Douvas · Kimberly Dowdell · Cornelius DuBois · Timothy Dufault · Tim Durfee Studio · Steve Durrant · John A Dutton, Dutton Architects · Duvall Decker Architects · Paul Eagle · Steven Ehrlich · Rand Ekman · Carl Elefante · Todd Enoki · John Enright · Michael Epp · Deborah Epstein · Tricia Esser · Jose Estevez · Peter Exley · Karen Fairbanks · Kelly Farrell · Glenn Fellows · Diane Filippi · Mattia Flabiano · Barbara Flammang · Anne Fletcher · Katie Flynn · Jason Forney · Caren Foster · James R. Foster · Catherine Fowlkes · Erika Franke · Jane Frederick · Daniel Freed · FreelandBuck · Daniel Friedman · Laurie E. Friedman · John Friedman Alice Kimm Architects · Mark Frisch · R. David Frum · Fung + Blatt Architects · Richard Furman · Louis Garapolo · Robert S. George · Katherine Georgeson · Diane Georgopulos · Margi Glavovic Nothard · Jeff Goldstein · Roger Goldstein · Dechen Gonnot · Nathan Good · Rob Goodwin · Gary Graham · Jennifer Graham · Emily Grandstaff-Rice · Frank Greene · Luanne Greene · Dina Griffin · Griffin Enright Architects · Mary Griffin · Francisco Grimaldi · Charlotte Grojean · Peter Grueneisen · Robin Guenther · Frank M. Guillot · Eric Haas · Harvey Hacker · Eric Haesloop · Michael Halflants · Ji Hye Ham · Michael Hamilton · William Hammer · William Harris · Sally Harrison · Michael Hass · David Hecht · Allison Held · Julie Hiromoto · Katherine Hogan & Vincent Petrarca, tonic design · Everett Hollander · Angel Hosband · Diane Hoskins · Alvin Huang, Synthesis Design + Architecture · Emily Huang · Bryan Hudson · Chris Hudson · Ted Hyman · Gregory S. Ibañez, Ibañez Shaw Architecture · Gregory Iboshi · Steve Imrich · Robert Ivy · Mark Jensen · Mike Jobes · Kenneth Johnson · Stephen Johnson · Casey Jones · Margo Jones · Alan Joslin · Michael Joyce · Bundit Kanisthakhon · Frank Karreman · Arlan Kay · Doug Kelbaugh · Gregory Kessler · Lia Kiladis · Wade Killefer · Julie Kim · Kari Kimura · Judith Kinnard · Kent Kleinman · Branko Kolarevic · Hank Koning & Julie Eizenberg · Philip Kramer · Amy Krasnow · Wendy Krum · Peter Kuttner · Nfn Kwendeche · Jeffrey Landman · Mary Ann Lazarus · Brian Lee · M. David Lee · Jane E. Lee · Sophia Lee · Andrea Leers · Mark Levine · Anne M. Lewis · Steven Lewis · Janice Li · Tom Liebel · Theodore Liebman · Karin Liljegren · Britt Lindberg · Liz's Antique Hardware · Melissa Lo · John Long · Luis Lopez-Baquero · Leslie Louden · Ivenue Love-Stanley · Bradley Lukanic · Paul Lukez · Rodolfo Machado · Peter MacKeith · Malcolm MacKenzie · Jean Mah · Matthew Malone · Michael Maltzan · Timothy Mansfield · Clark Manus · Richard Marshall · Emily Marthinsen · Liz Martin-Malikian · Marble Fairbanks Architects · Randall Masonn · Thom Mayne · Marsha Maytum, Leddy Maytum Stacy Architects · Susan McClymonds · Robert McConnell · Steve McConnell · Margaret McDonald · Zack McKown · Terence Meehan, Azimuth · Mitra Memari · Mike Mense · John Messervy · George Metzger · Juan Miró · Robert Misel · Melvin Mitchell · Robert Mitchell · Julia Monk · Montalba Architects · Anthony Montalto · Jonathan Moody · Stirling Morris · Lisa Mosier · Hubert Murray · Solvei Neiger · Brian Nelson · Karen L. Nelson · Sarah Nettleton · Catie Newell · Dan Noble · Peter Noone · Charles R. Norris · Diane Charyk Norris · Gregg Novicoff · John Nyfeler · Ed Ogosta · OJB Landscape Architects · John Olson · Chad Oppenheim · Lynn Osborn · Peter Papesch · David Parsons · Casius Pealer · Nicholas Peckham · Chris Pemberton · Alexander Perkins · Mark Peters · Michael Plottel · Monica Ponce de Leon · Catherine Popolow · Brad Prestbo · Robert Pulito · Mark Quattrocchi · Quattrocchi Kwok Architects · Stephen Quick · Ken Radtkey · Richard Radville · Leah Ray · Ralph Raymond · Sharon Refvem · Richard Renner · John S. Reynolds · David Rice · Patty Rice-Spivey · Yvette Richardson · Carolyn Rickard-Brideau · David Rifkind · Peter Robinson · Wendy Rogers · Anthony Rohr · Shaun Roth · Zigmund Rubel · William Ruhl · Karina Ruiz · Claudia Russell · Jenny Sabin · John Sadlon · Whitney Sander · Sanders Pace Architecture · Daniel Sandomire · Brian Sands · Yiselle Santos · Kathleen Schaefers · Jenny Scheu · Scott Schiamberg · Kenneth Schwartz · Warren Schwartz · Elissa Scrafano, Scrafano Architects · Jonathan Segal · Matthew Segal · Rebecca Seward-Beamer · Bart Shaw · Jessica Sheridan · Shimoda Design Group · Nushelle de Silva · Marc Simmons · Cathy Simon · Jonathan Sinagub · Jim Singleton · James Sink · SmartArchitecture · Anne Smith · Brenda Smith · Carlton Smith · Gabriel Smith · Mitchell Smith · Peter Smith · Raphael Sperry · Ross Spiegel · William J. Stanley III · Brian Staton · Allyn Stellmacher · Belinda Stewart · Todd Stine · Melody Stinson · Charles Stott · Larry Strain · Max Strang · Anson Stuart · Margaret Sullivan · Margaret Sullivan Studio · Katie Swenson · Keat C. Tan · Pamela Tang · Warren Techentin · Nader Tehrani · Robert Theel · Jim Theiss · Andrew Thompson · Barbara Thornton · Patrick Tighe · Douglas Tom · Mario Torroella · John Francis Torti · Theodore Touloukian · Trahan Architects · Nancy Rogo Trainer · Richard Tremaglio · Tom Trenolone · Franca Trubiano + Yves Gauthier in honor of Booker Taliaferro Washington, Robert R Taylor & Julian Abele · Calvin Tsao · Tulane School of Architecture · John Tumino · George Ellsworth Turnbull · Bruce Turner · Jay Valgora · Karen Van Lengen · David Varner · Randall Vaughn · Enrique Villa · Jim Vogel · Todd Voth · Ingalill Wahlroos-Ritter · Jan Wampler · Christina Wasch · Micki Washington · Dana Waymie · Jay Weber · Carole Wedge · Claire Weisz · Richard Whealan · Clive Wilkinson Architects · Amanda Williams · Beverly Willis · Michael Willis · Ashley Wilson · Walter Wilson · Allyne Winderman · Scott Wolf · James Woolum · Cole Wycoff · Jason Young · Joanne Young · Buzz Yudell · Ayo Yusuf · Willy Zambrano · Jeffrey Zutz · Frank Zwart.

The Architects Foundation's Diversity Advancement Scholarship supports minority students with a multi-year award towards their architectural education. This scholarship fund needs your support to increase diversity in the architecture profession at any NAAB-accredited school, especially at the seven accredited Historically Black Colleges and Universities.

Please consider making a generous donation at
architectsfoundation.org/hbcu
to help design a better future for all of us.

Project to raise funds for scholarships for minority students.
The New York Times *full page October 25, 2020.*

PART 3

Paul: So, let's talk about the additional influences that shaped your career, including encounters you've had with key architects as a young architect. I recall the story about your incredible encounter with Frank Lloyd Wright in Chicago. What made you decide to be an architect? What convictions fueled your career?

Jan: I moved from Marion, Ohio, to Meadville, Pennsylvania, with my mother and stepfather. The landscape was the opposite of Ohio, which had plains and no trees. In Meadville, I lived in the woods, basically, and I loved it. I'd spent hours out there exploring and building things. That may be when I started building bigger structures like huts. I was always designing houses in those days. I'm not sure who, if anyone, guided me but I remember that there were five books on architecture in the Meadville Public Library and I read all of them multiple times. One was about the Auditorium Building in Chicago by Dankmar Adler and Louis Sullivan. And there was one on international architecture. So that may have inspired me. Then I started working. In Pennsylvania you had to be 16 before you could work. So, I forged my papers to appear to be 16 when I was only 14. And I got my first job in an architect's office in Erie.

Paul: That's very young.

Jan: Yeah. I was the go-to guy. I did everything. I opened and closed the office, made prints, organized the library, and drew. I had to get up at six in the morning and hitchhike to Erie, Pennsylvania, about 40 miles and hitchhike back at night, getting home at eight or so.

The guidance of David Isaiah Goldberg, the firm's head, was decisive then. It was a small office, three people besides the partners. I did all the title blocks and I had to put his initials, DIG, on the drawings. Every night he would leave last and before leaving he'd come to my desk, sit down, and spend an hour showing me how to draw and talking about architecture when he should have been home with his family. I got an education from that. He would draw details of whatever I was drawing. He would sketch a detail on a piece of wood at a site and if he had to make a change order, I would draw up the detail. I remember that he would draw the section freehand without a scale. After he left, I would take a scale to it. I was amazed that it was in perfect scale. For some reason, and I don't know why, he took an interest in me. That was my first contact with an architect.

During the school year I also worked at several other jobs at the same time. In my little town, Meadville, I worked for a surveyor, where I was a draftsman, a lineman, a machete man and an instrument man. I did that on weekends. After school I worked for a contractor, doing takeoffs for his bids on projects and designing buildings for him. Those were the days before building codes were strictly followed and I'm not even sure there were building permits. It was much easier to get something built. Several years ago, I went back to PA and I looked at my buildings. They weren't bad. In fact, I was pleased with them.

By the time I entered RISD as a freshman I'd already had a lot of experience in the nuts and bolts of architecture. This caused me to go in the opposite direction, because I didn't want to be confined by knowing too much about the techniques of architecture. So, I did some outrageous things with the goal of experimenting.

I had those office jobs when I was in high school, summer jobs with architects and other jobs related to architecture. But I also had a weird job as a short-order cook at a little place called Stan's Dairy Bar. It was near Allegheny College in Meadville, and it was a hangout for students. Some of them got to know me, included me in their activities, and provided another layer of education. They exposed me to college events including Pete Seeger concerts.

Paul: Oh, really?

Jan: Yeah. This was during or soon after the McCarthy era when Pete couldn't find work because of his political views. He was blacklisted. So, he would perform at small schools like Allegheny College. I stayed up all night talking with him. We had a great relationship which lasted for years. The last time I saw him was at MIT in 2000.

Long before that he was writing a song for the 1976 World's Fair for which I was designing Boston's entry. The song was never performed because the World's Fair entry, sabotaged by Louise Day Hicks, didn't make it that far. But Pete was working on a song titled "The Interdependence of Man," with the message that our wellbeing depends on connections with others. The central point of our design for the World's Fair was to use the money to address urgent social problems around the world, I think Pete was interested because of the alignment with his own values.

I was not a very good student in high school. In fact, I was a terrible student. I never did what I was supposed to. I had my own agenda, my own curriculum. I read a lot and broadly. Not just architecture: I read anything I could get my hands on and this would send me in new directions, spark new ideas. At night, instead of doing homework, I read. Consequently I didn't get good grades. I distinctly remember talking to the student guidance person.

Paul: Guidance counselor?

Jan: Yeah. He said, "You have no chance of getting into any college. Why don't you just continue working?" Which pissed me off, of course. The Allegheny College students apparently talked about me to some of their faculty, resulting in those faculty writing recommendations for me. There's a theme to this. I've always had incredibly good luck with people looking out for me or helping me.

Paul: Where did you apply?

Jan: I applied to Pratt, Carnegie, Penn State and Rhode Island School of Design/RISD. I visited Pratt, Penn State and Carnegie. Carnegie seemed to be all about fraternities, a scene I wanted nothing to do with. Pratt and Penn just didn't feel right for me. So, I decided to go to RISD, the one school I had not visited. I figured, well, what the hell, the others are not for me.

Paul: And did you apply to all these schools to study architecture or general admission?

Jan: Specifically, to study architecture. So high school was a disaster for me. I didn't like it. But I did like all the other things I did in pursuit of self-education. That was my method of operation at RISD too. But first, getting there — traveling to RISD from Meadville — felt unreal, like a good dream. I traveled all night on the train with my suitcase and typewriter. It took 24 hours then, as I went through New York. I remember arriving at the Providence RI train station. I was proud of myself that I'd gotten that far. As I said earlier, my stepfather had passes on the railroads so I could travel anywhere for free. Going to RISD was more complicated than my earlier trips to New York and Chicago, but I loved this journey, and it took me to the place where I saw the ocean for the first time.

At RISD I ended up in a house with 12 other guys. I had a little room in the attic. I had no money. That is another ongoing theme of my life: never had much money. I worked to pay for school. I worked my way through school. RISD felt like heaven. Everyone was an oddball, so I fit in and had a wonderful first year. I think what they call Freshman Foundation is an incredible grounding for people going into the design fields. As you probably know, RISD is all design. I painted and sculpted. At the time it was a place for non-conformists and outliers, and I enjoyed that. However, my second year, when I got into architecture, was somewhat of a disappointment.

Paul: Why?

Jan: Well, local practitioners taught the studios, and they seemed unenthusiastic about doing it. But something that was great about the architecture program: the administration allocated funds to bring inspiring architects to RISD. That's where I met Louis Kahn.

I remember staying up all night with him. He'd give a lecture, but the best part was what happened afterwards. We would go to somebody's house after the lecture and talk late into the night. This was wonderful. I met Louis Kahn, Paul Rudolph, Philip Johnson, Richard Neutra and Bruce Goff. Neutra once had lunch at my small, gritty apartment.

Bruce Goff was wacky as hell. He was great. My stock went way up after he came because I was doing wacky things. But Bruce Goff was doing more outlandish things than I was. So suddenly people were saying, "Hey, you know, what you're doing might be okay." However I hope I never have students who are the kind of student I was then.

At RISD, I continued to pursue my own self-designed curriculum. I constructed things — I guess you would call it architecture or sculptures — and set them out around Rhode Island in various places, maybe 15 or 20 installations made of concrete, glass, plaster, steel, or wood. And then I would go back to see how nature worked on them.

I remember being excited when I went back to a piece made of concrete or plaster on poles and found green moss growing on its north side. I found a bird's nest in another metal piece. And when I revisited one I did in a cornfield, the farmer had ploughed around it. I always wondered if he thought it came from aliens.

While at RISD I worked at many different jobs. I was the draftsman at a place making cabinets and furniture. The building was four or five stories high. They would start at the top, making the cabinet, and work all the way down to painting it on the lowest floor. I would follow it every day to see my work as it went down.

I learned a lot about how to put stuff together there. I was the hippie, bohemian or whatever, but the workers appreciated me despite our differences. I was something of a smart-ass. One day I expressed irritation at the conventional colonial style. "That's not modern," I'd say. So, the principal said, "Okay, here's a job for you. We're doing a bank and we're doing counters. Why don't you design the counters?" I thought, "Holy shit!"

Paul: Wow!

Jan: I worked day and night, putting in much more time than I was paid and boy, did I design those counters. They were made of marble and teak wood, simple but elegant. I thought they were great, and the principal did too. It was a whole new thing for me. On the day of assembly, I was there, and I remember my stomach churning when I realized I hadn't measured the door width. There was no way they could get in. He saw it at the same time. And he was cool. He said, "Well, we're going to install them on another day. We have some finishing touches to do." I wasn't there but apparently; they took down part of the wall at night and got the counters in.

I thought, "I'm in big trouble now. I'm gonzo." When I reported for work the next afternoon, I figured that was going to be my end there. I went by his office, and he yelled at me: "Hey, kiddo, get in here!" And he said, "If you ever make something again, and don't measure the door, you're history!" Then he added, "The client loves them." To this day I still measure doors.

Paul: Those are valuable lessons.

Jan: I had a lot of those on-site lessons. But anyway, that was a great experience. The bigger experience was working for William D. Warner, an architect. I worked for Bill when he was in Providence, in a little room. I was the only person he hired at that time. We did houses, schools and rehabs of houses. The biggest project was on Cape Cod and is now called New Seaberry, a second-home community. One of the first. I worked on the design of the canals and some of the architecture. He also sent me down there to supervise the crane operator who was digging the canals. The crane guy would take me in his bucket way up high so I could see where we were going. It was an amazing experience.

Paul: For sure.

Jan: But there was another lesson in that experience, I came back saying, "Hey, we can't do this. We're destroying the habitat of so many animals, fish, and vegetation." For me that was the beginning of ecological awareness, although I didn't know it by that name. I was upset that every day we were destroying habitats of living creatures. But overall, it was a great experience, including supervising that and other projects. I worked for Bill for four years, during the school year and in the summers. He was a great architect.

Paul: He was a very accomplished architect. And, of course, Bill did the famous urban design project in Providence, where he created a rich network of bridges and public spaces.

Jan: Then he moved his office to the mill and designed a house for himself on the land. I learned a lot from Bill. He was a very careful designer. He worked hard at it. I may have gotten the ability to work hard from him.

Paul: You were lucky to have had parallel educational tracks in your training as an architect — one academic, the other professional. As you were going through educational programs in high school or at RISD, you were also rooted in a professional set of experiences with professional practices.

Jan: Yes. I had both sides, so to speak.

Paul: And what's interesting about the way you developed your training as an architect is that you grounded your design work in an understanding of the technical aspects of construction, building systems, etc. Perhaps this freed you up to explore designs in a way that was informed by reality knowing how far you could push design ideas.

Jan: Yeah. The problem is, I was a bit of a rebel which jeopardized my academic standing. This was during the days when, if you didn't maintain a certain average, you were A-1 and ready to go to Vietnam, but you got deferment while you were in school. But I did manage to maintain it — I don't remember if it was a B or a B-plus average.

Paul: What a dilemma.

Jan: For one design studio I went to a site in Rhode Island, a south-facing site on the ocean, where the assignment was to design a $5 million house for a prominent lawyer whose wife liked to collect art. After sleeping on the site, I went back and announced in class that I wouldn't do the project because the land was too beautiful to be ruined by a piece of architecture for people who didn't deserve it. Instead, I would design a state park there. Of course, I flunked that one. That meant the next time I had to work my ass off to get an A+ to keep my average up. I'm not badmouthing RISD. I loved RISD. I loved the people I met there, some of whom are still good friends.

Someone of huge importance from my RISD years and beyond was a young faculty member named Ernie Kerwin. Until his death a few years ago he was a mentor, guide, friend and touchstone. Coincidentally he was an MIT graduate. He thought highly of me and took me under his wing.

He said I was either insane or a genius; he didn't know which. Next to the Market House, which housed RISD's architecture department, was a piece of land where they had an annual exhibition, probably to gain visibility and raise money for the department.

Ernie was responsible for appointing someone to design the exhibition which sophomores or juniors would build. The exhibits were typically little Japanese gardens with paintings and sculpture. Though my constructions were unconventional, one year Ernie selected me to design the exhibit. I didn't want to do one of those little Japanese kinds of place. I have nothing against Japanese architecture unless it's pulled out of Japan and placed elsewhere. But I wanted to create something different, that an architect, painter, sculptor, and ceramicist could do together.

I picked glass as the medium. This was before the days of glassblowing at RISD. I found a guy at MIT Lincoln Labs who blew glass forms for the moon program. Somehow, he got me into this top-secret place and taught me how to blow glass. We would blow unusual forms based on our individual visions. I experimented with other materials too. I was making pylons around this open space, out of sand with a magic material called AM9, which was invented to stabilize oil wells. I don't know how but somehow, I got them to contribute a truckload of this stuff, which was a chemical you mixed with water. I thought I would pour it into the forms and then students could carve into it. I experimented with it in the chemistry or physics lab and made forms and subjected them to pressure and the elements. It worked fine in the lab. However, it didn't work well in reality. So, I had a whole truckload of AM9 that I stored in the basement of the Market House. That summer a major hurricane flooded the Market House and turned the basement into Jell-O. That did not endear me to the RISD administration.

Anyway, I took the glass forms, placed them in plateaus, and made prisms, mirrors, and a lens. I put those on all the buildings around the site, each focused on a particular form and timed to turn a color when the sun hit it. That was my first project that was published, in an Italian magazine.

To address the fact that at night the area was kind of dullsville I had lights in the bottom of a tube, and a lens. The light would go up the tube and explode into the form. Then I found an old piano player and I wrote a composition by connecting the wires from forms to each key on the piano so the light would go on and off. I learned to play the piano. I didn't have money, so the whole thing had to rely on cheap extension cords. I could have electrocuted an elephant. The Providence Building Code shut it down. Still, we had showings at 3AM since I had the keys connected to the circuits so I could play the piano and turn the forms into light.

Paul: You were already interested in finding ways in which your interest in music could be translated into other art forms?

Jan: Well, yes. I've always been interested in the relationship between music and architecture. Still am exploring it. At RISD I had a music course for which we were told to write an essay about a musical piece. Instead, I did it with forms of light from a show of forms moving through space. That's what started the glass garden idea. Those glass forms may still be stashed in a building at RISD. I've never gone back to see if they're there. There were probably 200 of them.

Then it came time for my thesis. At that time, the thesis was supposed to show your ability to be an architect, which meant electrical, structural, mechanical knowledge and design. If you were an average student, it was suggested that you do a high school, because that was when we were starting to build schools for the baby-boomers. If you were a good student, perhaps an embassy, because we were building embassies all over the world then. And if you were an exceptional student, you got to do a church, because a church was seen as the highest form of architecture. I didn't want to do any of those.

I had learned that in Nova Scotia people who built boats and fished didn't have adequate housing. The Canadian government was sending in trailers which no one wanted. So, for my thesis I decided to go to Nova Scotia in my beat-up old car, a Morris Minor which I bought for $55. (I never put more than a dollar's worth of gas in it because

I didn't know when it was going to fall apart.) I drove it to Maine to the place where the boat left for Yarmouth. My girlfriend pilfered a bunch of egg-salad sandwiches from the cafeteria for me to take as sustenance. They froze, because there was no heat in the car which was a permanent convertible since the top wouldn't go up. It was winter, probably January, and I would put the sandwiches on top of the engine block to heat them for dinner.

I went to Yarmouth and explored that part of Nova Scotia. I finally found a little village, where there were boat-builders and fishermen. It was very cold. I quickly learned that I could have myself arrested and put in jail where I could get dinner, breakfast and a warm place to stay. I'd go to the jail or to a cop on the street, and say, "I think you should arrest me" or something like that. Thinking I was crazy, they would arrest me, and take me to jail where I got dinner, a place to sleep, and breakfast.

They kept me there until the children were in school, in case I was a threat, I guess. Eventually I found a small town and was given a place to stay in return for doing a bit of everything. I swept the floors of the boat-building place. I worked as a hand on the boats. I don't know if you know about the tides there. They are very high. You drove out on flats where there was water, there were nets, and you could pick the fish off the nets. At low tide, of course — 20-foot tides.

So, I worked there and then designed a village for them, and housing. Then I returned to RISD a few weeks before final thesis reviews. With a bunch of friends, I built a huge model of the village I had designed. The drawings were all on yellow trace paper. But the standard then was to draw with ink on illustration board and then, believe it or not, with a ruling pin. But mine were all sketches. You had to show mechanicals. So, for electricity I made a drawing of a gas lamp because that was the town's source of light. For plumbing, I drew an outhouse because that was their plumbing. For heating, I drew a stove.

I vividly remember sitting outside the room while the jury was deciding what grade I would get. I can see them opening the door and walking by me, not saying a word. And I looked in and saw a big red F over a little A.

Paul: Oh, wow. What was the A?

Jan: Ernie Kerwin, my teacher and friend. But I flunked, I flunked out.

Paul: Oh, my God. Were you surprised?

Jan: I was, yes.

Paul: But you also knew that you were pushing the —

Jan: — envelope. Oh, yeah, I was pushing the envelope, as always. I thought, "Oh, God, here I am about to get married with a baby on the way, and I'm not going to graduate, I don't have a job, what the hell am I going to do?" Before that, I had met Carl Lynn who came to RISD to give a lecture and who worked as a professor at UPenn. He and I became friends. He was building tot-lots or playgrounds in Philadelphia for underprivileged kids. I'd go down there on weekends and work with him. He was getting a program for Boston to do the same thing. He suggested, since he didn't have the grant yet — and he never got the money, by the way — that I get a job with the Boston Redevelopment Authority. Great man, wonderful man.

I came to Boston where I was interviewed at the BRA by David Crane, who was a professor at UPenn. He hired me. Years later, I asked his administrative assistant, "Why did David Crane give me a job?" He had hired a bunch of Penn grads and here I was a RISD guy. She said, "Dave always talked about you. He believed you had something to offer." What it was I never knew. I started working there though I hadn't graduated from RISD.

That changed when Albert Bush-Brown became president of RISD. As the story goes, they were showing him around the architecture department. My thesis model, which I'd built in the exhibition room, was so big that they couldn't get rid of it. So, they built a wall around it and left it there. When he saw it, he asked what it was. They said, "It was made by this guy who never graduated and is gone now." Bush-Brown said, "I'd like to have this as a model and design to show what we're doing here." When they told him I hadn't graduated he replied, "That's no problem."

Soon after, I got a call from the president's office — not for the first time: I'd been arrested often in Providence and jailed for things like running down the street when it was cold, mistaken for a thief. I thought, "Oh, God, what have I done now?" Summoned to RISD, I walked into Bush-Brown's office where he shook my hand, handed me my diploma, and offered me a teaching job. It was hard for me to believe that this was happening.

Paul: Then you graduated from RISD and then you went on to work for the BRA, right?

Jan: Yes, but while I was there, I was accepted at Harvard GSD, so I was in graduate school at the same time. Now, at the BRA during that time, I met Aldo Van Eyck. I didn't know who Aldo was in his early days. He had built the Amsterdam Orphanage, but he wasn't internationally recognized yet. He'd done a lot for children in Amsterdam. My assignment was the South End. I had an overall plan of building play yards, daycare centers, health centers, garden centers and other facilities the community needed. Dave Crane called me to his office one day and said, "We have an expert coming from Europe who's taking over what you're doing." That irritated me, so I kept going back into his office, asking "Why do we have to depend on experts from Europe, for God's sake?"

Finally, I went back in, and he said, "Okay, tell you what: Put your drawings up in the conference room, everything you've done, and you can present to this expert who's coming." I said, "Okay." He added, "On one condition: you don't slam my door when you go out." Which I didn't. I covered the conference room with my work, and the next day when I went into the conference room there was Aldo. He was doing something I used to do: I always had a cup of coffee in my hand which I would stir with a 314 Berol pencil with a lot of sugar in it, then lick the sugar off the pencil. This may explain some of my problems! It was a way of getting my pencil clean. Aldo was doing the same thing.

I thought, "I wonder what this guy is up to." I presented my work to him and others in the room, and he gave me the best critique of my life. He said things like "When you do this, think about moving this over a little bit more." Finally, he got up and said to Dave, "You don't need me. You have Jan." Then I got up and said, "No, we do need you." So, Aldo invited me to go to lunch with him, and we did. I still remember Dave sitting there with his head in his hands, saying, "I don't understand architects."

That was the beginning of a long rich relationship with Aldo. I'm not sure how I got admitted to Harvard, but Aldo had a role. As part of the application process, I asked if he would mind filling out a recommendation form. Aldo took the form, put it on the corridor wall, and wrote (to the attention of Jose Sert, at the time Dean of the GSD) "José, take him. If you don't, you will be sorry."

Paul: Were you at the BRA for two years?

Jan: Yes, but I also worked at the BRA when I went to Harvard. I worked 35 hours a week, because I had a wife and new daughter.

Paul: My God. And going to school at the same time.

Jan: Yes, I would go to a class, then take the MBTA to City Hall and work for a couple of hours, and then take the MBTA back to GSD for a class. Once I went out to get a coffee and forgot what I was doing — and took the T to Boston for no reason.

Paul: So you were getting no sleep.

Jan: Yeah, no sleep. My GSD classmates were all international. The connections have lasted. I'm still friends with many of them. Two died recently. It's very sad. We have been meeting every year for the past decade. Well, not during COVID, but we had reunions in countries including Japan, Spain, Austria. The GSD was wonderful. I loved the experience. It was Jersey Solton, Sert, Jacky Tyrwhitt, Shad Woods and Maki.

Paul: That's great. And you were studying urban design?

Jan: It was urban design. God, it was just wonderful— intense, vibrant in a way that RISD hadn't been for me. At Harvard, there were people passionate about ideas, who talked about them and encouraged you to do so. I was thinking about this the other day, that these poor kids who went to school during COVID never had the experience of being in a studio as well as other benefits of being there in person. Some of my best talks at Harvard in the old Robinson Hall were in the hallway with Sert and other faculty. It was a wonderful education and Sert was so helpful to me.

Paul: In which ways?

Jan: For one thing, trying to find me a job in South America.

Paul: So, you had wanted to go and work in South America?

Jan: Yes.

Paul: And what drew you to going to South America?

Jan: At that young age, on my first international trip to Europe, I went to Rome where I met up with a friend. He wanted to show me the Colosseum. I said, "I don't want to see the Colosseum. I want to see where people are living. Poor people." I was interested in housing for the underprivileged. South America offered that opportunity. The problem is, there was no money. I went to Lima, Caracas and Bogota in search of work. All had terrible housing problems but no money to do anything. I ended up in Puerto Rico, because Puerto Rico had the same problems, but they also had money to do something about it. I ended up there by accident — it hadn't been my first choice.

Paul: Interesting.

Jan: I was there for three years.

Paul: So, you went from Harvard to Puerto Rico.

Jan: Correct.

Paul: And straight out of school, when you went to Puerto Rico, did you go work for an agency?

Jan: Yes, I was working for ARUV, Administration of Urban Renewal and Housing. They were the housing agency for Puerto Rico. I think the way it worked is that they were getting an urban renewal grant from the US. In that grant — I didn't know this at the time — you had to have a design section. Puerto Rico didn't have one, so they hired me to do that. I started by myself, but by the end of two years half a dozen people were working with me.

Paul: You speak Spanish?

Jan: I spoke Spanish then, yes, learned on the job. I never had a Spanish language course. Instead, I learned it in the slum where I worked because many didn't speak English.

Paul: And so, you were there for two and a half years. Did you see any of the projects get built?

Jan: Yes, I did many kinds of projects and received some awards.

Paul: The Progressive Architecture award.

Jan: The PA Design Award, First Place, which was another one of those things I never expected. That's how I got to MIT because the dean of the MIT School of Architecture and Planning, Andy (Lawrence) Anderson was chair of the PA jury. He fought for my project and after that invited me to have sherry with him at MIT. I did, and we had a good talk for an hour. Months later someone called from his office asking for my Social Security number. I wondered why. She said, "Because you're going to teach here." I said, "What do you mean? I didn't know there was a job, and I've never been interviewed." She replied, "Of course you were interviewed. That's why you met with Andy several months ago." That's how I got to MIT. Complete fluke.

But going back to Puerto Rico, I did something called Vivenda Experimental, which was a project for experimental housing. We built some prototypes at that time. They had tried bringing in Bucky Fuller's geodesic domes for housing, but that had been a disaster because it was so hot, probably the worst thing you could do there. People hated it!

Paul: Where did you live? Did you live in the old town?

Jan: I lived in the old city, in an old Spanish house.

Paul: The old city was amazing, wasn't it?

Jan: Well, there were no tourists to speak of then. Now it's overrun with tourists. It's become an "in" place to be, which is why they were going to relocate La Perla to the outskirts, because they wanted to build up the tourist industry. La Perla, a shanty town, was not part of the plan. It was a poor place, and it was dangerous. I later lived in La Perla for a short time. I loved Puerto Rico, the people, and working there.

Paul: What brought you back to the States again?

Jan: I was determined to save my marriage. My wife had left me and gone back to Boston. At first, I would come on weekends. Then I realized I had to move back but I did not have a job in Boston, so I called the BRA and asked if they had any openings. They said, "There is a job to draw a perspective to use for public relations for Boston's entry in the 1976 World's Fair competition and I said, "I'll take it." I was desperate. That's how I got into designing the World's Fair.

Paul: That was a temporary job? Or was it a permanent job?

Jan: It was a permanent job. I was there for another three years. Someone had already done a design for the World's Fair, based on New York's '64 World's Fair. It was essentially, US Royal Tires does a Ferris wheel in the shape of a giant tire, and other silly pavilions. I wanted to see if I could take an approach that would help to solve urban problems.

Ed Logue was the director of the BRA. I met with him to ask if I could use a different approach. I said I needed two weeks to develop the idea. He said OK but gave me just ten days. At the end of ten days, I presented the idea, which was to use the World's Fair as a laboratory for solving urgent global problems related to transportation, food, housing, education, health, water etc. Each country and industry would take a topic and show what they have done and future research directions. All this would be exhibited at the Fair. Some structures would be reused for new housing in Boston.

Finally, Ed looked at me, said, "OK" and asked what I wanted. I told him I wanted to hire a half-dozen architect/planner friends, have a budget for materials and a place to work that was not in the City Annex. He okayed that too. Then I asked if I could have a good hi-fi system to listen to the Beatles all day while we worked. He said, "Get out of here." I had pushed it too far. So, we worked at 178 Atlantic Ave secretly for several years. Philadelphia was in the competition. So was Miami, of all places. I think I was given the 178 Atlantic building partly because they didn't have room at the City Hall and largely to keep me hidden.

Paul: Was that on one of the wharves?

Jan: Yeah, that's one of the wharf buildings. Right on the water. It was going to be torn down.

Paul: Yeah. You were very lucky. You got to see some of old Boston before so much of it was torn down.

Jan: Oh, yeah. Well, I saw the West End before it was torn down.

Paul: What a loss.

Jan: Yeah. The West End was a huge loss.

Paul: That's incredible. How much time did you have to design it?

Jan: A year and a half, something like that. We made this huge model I've been told is still somewhere in the City Hall.

The model showed what the area looked like at present. Then you pressed a button, and it would turn over and show our World's Fair idea; then you pressed another button, and it showed how the new city would look afterwards.

Paul: Remarkable.

Jan: The idea was to reuse the structures afterwards. This raised another issue. I presented it to the City Council, including calculations for how much money could be saved by using the World's Fair for a new city for housing. I don't know how precise my calculations were, but I said, "You could save millions of dollars" to which they responded "Kid, you don't get it. We want to get the money to build it, then we want to get the money to tear it down."

Paul: That's crazy. It's a completely different way of thinking about urban design than how we think about sustainability today. You were way ahead of the curve. You think about the London Olympics, and the World Cup in Qatar. Those venues are focused on reusing or recycling different elements that are part of the stadium or ancillary buildings.

Jan: Well, it turned out to be a competition between Philadelphia, Boston and Miami. We presented to the World's Fair committee in Washington. It was a two or three-day ordeal presenting to the committee, but it was also the bad time of the Vietnam War, and Nixon was in. And, as you know, there was no World's Fair in 1976. I think there was so much disruption in this country that they decided to can the whole thing. Also, because ex-president Kennedy was the one who had come up with the idea of a 1976 World's Fair.

And there was Louise Day Hicks.

She was racist, and she didn't want the World's Fair because it meant black people would be on the subway going through South Boston. She protested big-time. She and I locked horns after one of the TV stations did an hour-long program on the World's Fair and interviewed me. I talked about how this could be an opportunity to solve big problems in the world. I said, "Doctors say if we could coordinate all the research on cancer, we could find a cure. This may be an opportunity to do that." The TV station spliced her in saying, "We'll never have the World's Fair here. It's a horrible idea. It has no use." Immediately after that they had me talking about solving cancer, which made her look bad.

Paul: Exactly.

Jan: She was very embarrassed by that. She wanted to be Mayor. The City Council was scared that if they approved the fair and she got to be mayor, they might lose her support. So, they didn't support it at all. Well, some did, but not all.

La Puntilla, San Juan, Puerto Rico

View of La Perla shacks outside the walls of Old San Juan

View of garbage and hogs at the water's edge

View of Old San Juan

Public space in Old San Juan

Children of La Perla

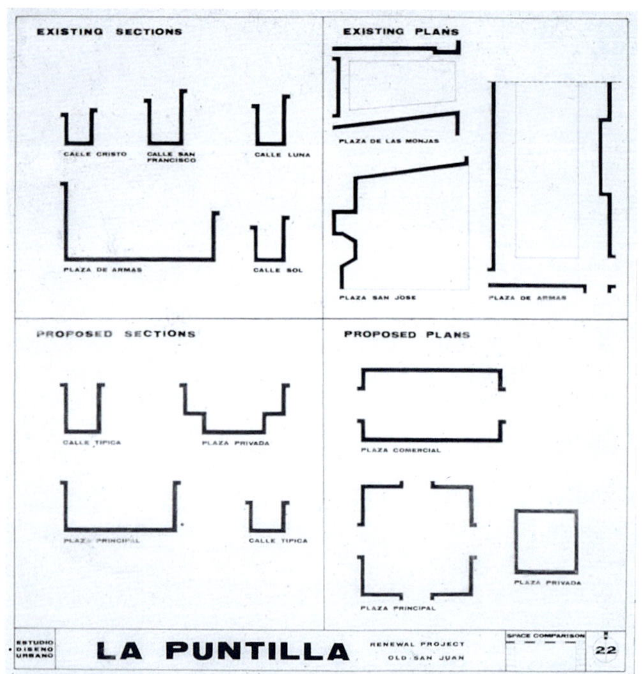

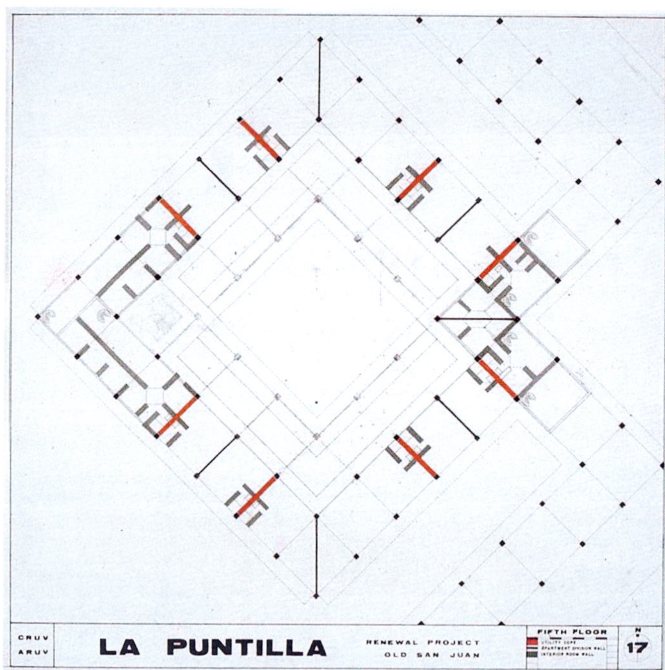

Public space in La Puntilla

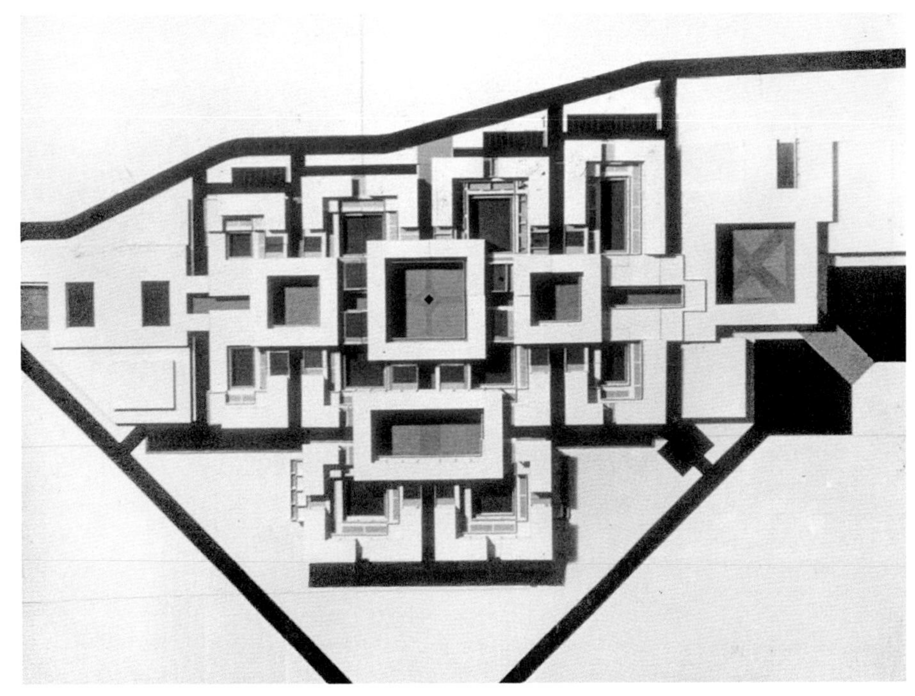

Model of La Puntilla Proposal

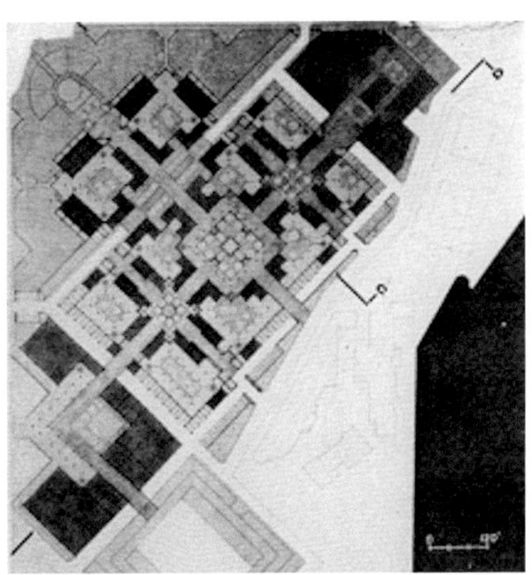

Floor Plans of La Puntilla Proposal

Views of public spaces in La Puntilla Proposal

Aerial view of La Perla outside wall of Old San Juan

Small plaza providing central water supply, Aguadilla, Puerto Rico. Children always at my side, while walking through barrio. 1966.

Movement Systems in the City
Boston, Mass.

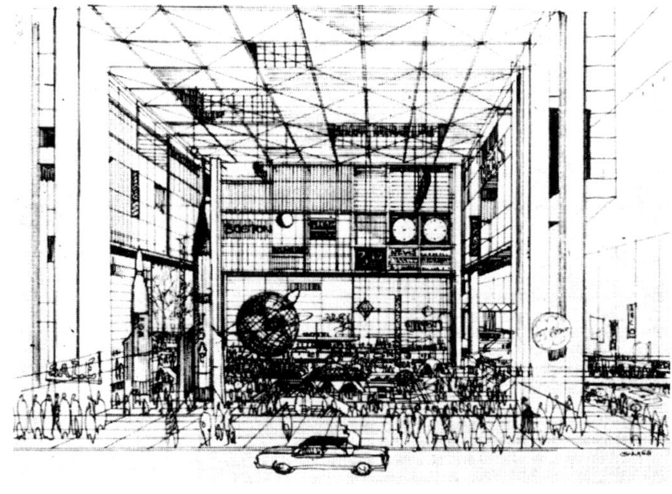

Proposal for City Room, Boston, MA.

Movement Systems in the City

by FUMIHIKO MAKI
with MARIO COREA
EDUARDO LOZANO
GUSTAVO MUNIZAGA
IAN WAMPLER

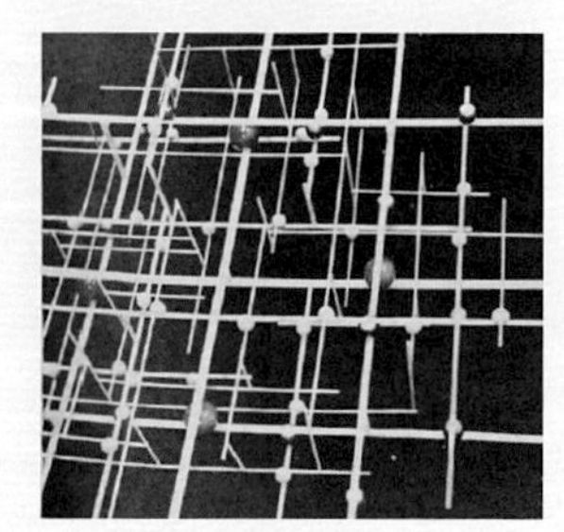

In spite of the recently emerging interest in the art and science of urban design, there have only been sporadic attempts to establish a methodology of the design tools essential to organizing both existing cities and those of the future. Without this basic vocabulary we have no systematic approach to organizing a framework for human habitat. The scale and complexity of contemporary events, as well as the enormity of those contemplated in the future, make the recognition of this need imperative to the very survival of our cities.

Within this concern it is the urban designer who must seek to establish three-dimensional spaces, precipitated by the events and activities of urban life, and viable in time sequences. The operation of the urban designer thus depends primarily on understanding those forces which exist, and among them recognizing and giving definition to those that hold meaning for the future. Without this understanding urban design becomes meaningless, and proceeds in terms unrelated to the underlying structure of society. At the same time, if urban design in satisfying utilitarian concerns ignores the human condition, the process becomes equally meaningless. The final result must be concerned with the human activity of the city.

Thesis Project
Nova Scotia

Seaside of new village in Nova Scotia

View of fish industry

View of new village

Glass Garden RISD
Providence, R.I.

Garden of light, glass and music
RISD, Providence, R.I. 1961. Images by Charles Arnold - RISD

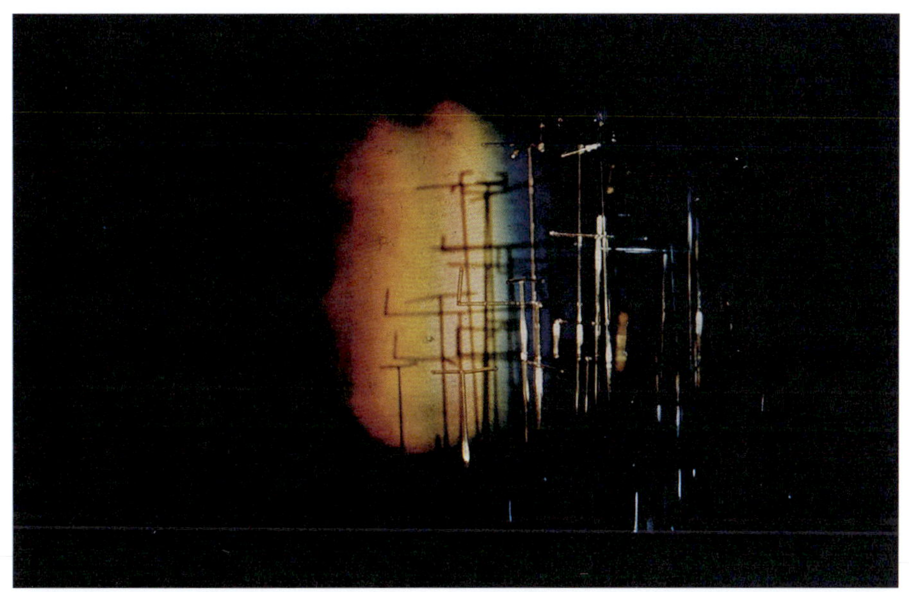

Glass Garden with color from mirrors and lens on glass form.
RISD, Providence, R.I. 1961. Images by Charles Arnold - RISD

Forms in Nature
RISD, Providence, R.I.

Forms placed in nature near Providence, R.I.

International Exposition 1976
Boston, MA

Pavilion of medical research in the world

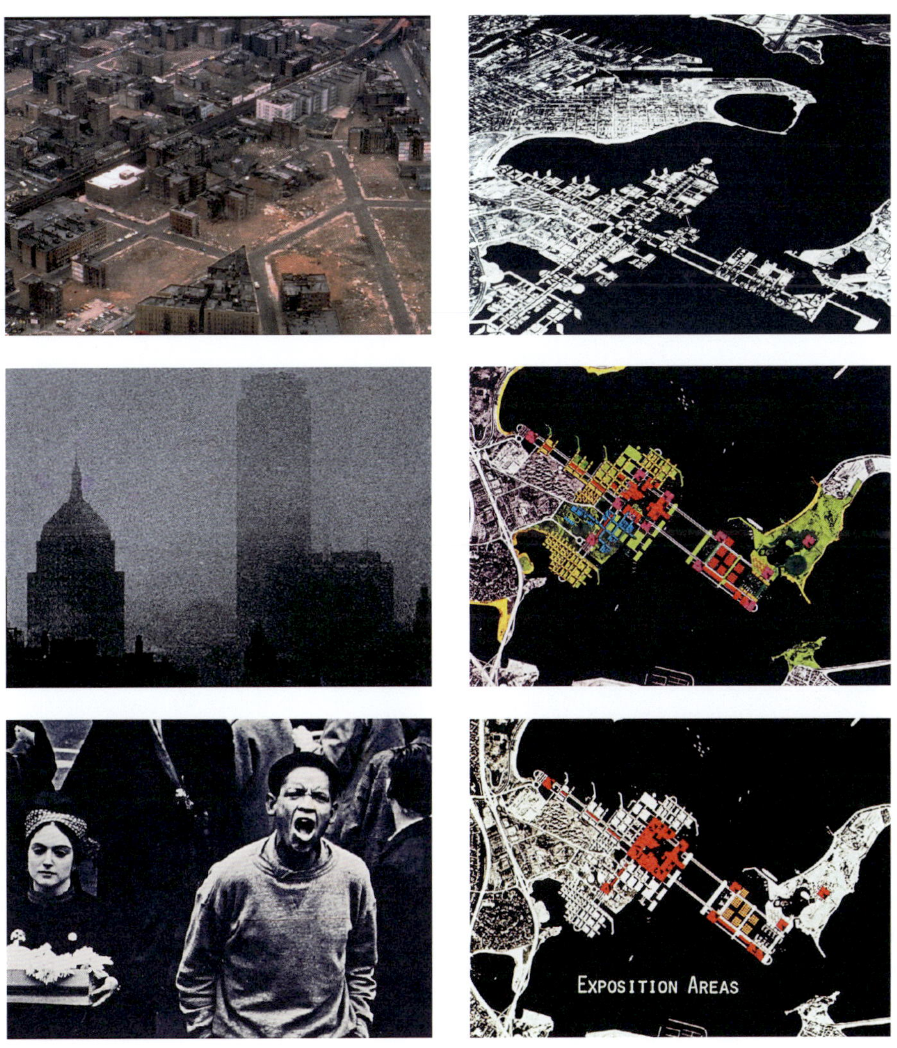

Social and physical problems of the world

Plans of World Fair

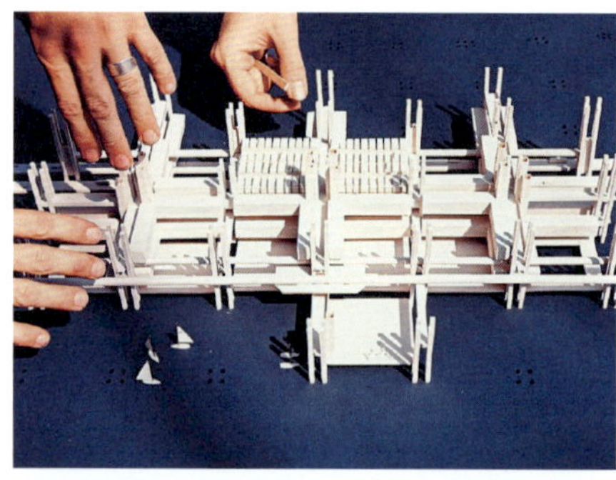

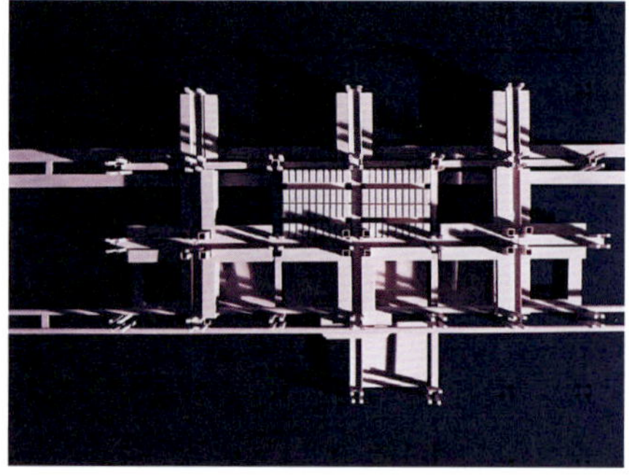

Model of how infrastructure would be used after World Fair is over

Views of Water Plaza

Living Alone

they live amongst the
garbage from the rich
of the city above
    moving back and forth
    with the tide
    bottles, bags, sewage,
    floating in the ocean

they live without clean water
drinking water from the city
above
    dirty, full of disease, gray
    sometimes sewage

they live in small houses
in contrast to the city above
    hot, many people
    to a room
    with newspapers to
    cover walls

they live with the threat
of a storm
while young Americans
surf the waves
    their house destroyed
    in minutes
    with the fury of the wind
but they build again
with imagination
and endurance
    more than the people
    who live above
    who do not have
    the skills
        of survival.
            for they know the
            ways of life

Contrasts

while some children
wake in the day
    to play, go to school
    to enjoy the day
    full of wonderment of life

while many children of the
world wake the day
    asking how they will eat
    suffering with illness
    working long hours for
    survival

while we live in a world of
contrasts
    with some with so much
    with most with so little

it is our task to find ways
    of making the world of
children
    of a better place for all
children

Priorities

while some are concerned
about beautiful clothes
    others
    only want cover from the
    cold

while some are concerned
about the correct food for a party
    others
    only want food for the
    night meal

while some are concerned
about beautiful architecture
    others
    only want to shelter
    the soul and body

can we work and live with
these contrasts
    without making their
    problems
    our problems

PART 4

Paul: So here we are with Jan Wampler. This is Paul Lukez, and this is a continuation of interview sessions we've had for a forthcoming book about Jan and his career. What we're going to do is pick up where we left off, which was a discussion of Jan being hired by Andy Anderson at MIT. Andy Anderson was the dean who had seen Jan's award-winning work as part of the PA awards jury submitted for a project he did in Puerto Rico.

So, Jan, this is a chance for us to talk about two sets of topics, and I think they're interrelated, because some of them were happening concurrently, and that is your career at MIT as an academic, a full-time professor. And at the same time, your engagement and practice, continuing the work you had done in Puerto Rico and at the BRA. Maybe you can frame for us what it was like to be engaged in those two sets of activities and then focus on whatever topic you prefer to tackle first and give us more about your impressions of what that was like.

Jan: Okay. Thanks. Well, first, when I was at the BRA before I began teaching at MIT, I had an office in Harvard Square in the old McCartney garage building. There were three people in the office, and I had several projects. The office had weird hours. It was open from 8PM until midnight. And it was open on Saturday and Sunday mornings.

We did several projects. One was for migratory workers in an apple orchard. A client wanted a design for housing for them. And that was built. I did a project for a man in Georgia, who did research showing that people's lifespans were shortened when they didn't have adequate sanitation, water or electricity. So, I designed something called the Health Core. It consisted of solar panels for energy, a water tank, toilet, kitchen facilities and self-contained sewage system.

There'd be a truck that would come, a sewage tank that removed waste, because there was no sewage system — a small kitchen sink and a refrigerator. It was very small, and prefabricated. It could be pushed up against an existing house so you could open a door where a window was and add it. You also could take it apart into four pieces and use it as the center of a new house. I worked on that, and it was published.

We worked on half a dozen different projects — housing, rehab and commercial. Then I was asked to do a rehab of Columbia Point housing — public housing.

Paul: Was that through a bid process, or were you just asked to do it?

Jan: I was asked by someone familiar with my work. I agreed to do it and I did. But then I started getting phone calls from the mayor's office asking how much I was donating to the campaign. I testified in City Council that this was going on. Those were not good days for me. I was upset that they gave me the commission, then thought I should pay them for it. Anyway, the Columbia Point project was interesting. They had money to rehab bathrooms, put in showers and install tile. After doing those things I had a little money left, enough to rehab one building. I took 10 Monticello, in Columbia Point, and redesigned it to meet residents' needs. I interviewed all the people who might live there. I found that there was no such thing as the typical American family of 2.8 people, happily married with kids. In fact, it was the opposite: no uniformity, no standard format. All kinds of different conditions. One model was two women who would join forces and buy food together because it was cheaper to buy and cook it together. They might have seven or eight kids between them. I designed an apartment for them. That project received another PA award.

Paul: Impressive!

Jan: I worked on that and did a complete set of CDs for it. It had to be approved by the Boston Housing Authority. I still remember going to them — I was in my 20's, young, naive— and presenting the plan. And they said "Hey, kiddo, you don't understand. If we do this, it would be great; we would like something like this for ourselves! But if we do it with one building, everyone will want it. We can't let that happen." So that was the end of that project. They didn't let it go through.

Paul: How many years did you do that before you started teaching at MIT? Was that like two or three years?

Jan: Three years, I would say.

Paul: It was after you went to Harvard Graduate School of Design and before you started MIT.

Jan: Right. I had come back from Puerto Rico. I was working at the same time on the World's Fair at the BRA. Also, I bought my house in Jamaica Plain then.

Paul: And you were on a tenure track.

Jan: Tenure track, yes.

Paul: What year was that? In the 1970s?

Jan: Yes, I started at MIT in 1970. And bought the house at the same time.

Paul: So an average house at the time cost $15,000 to $17,000.

Jan: The reason I could buy Kenton Road was because MIT paid from July to July. So, in September I got a check for two- or three-months' salary that I didn't expect. It was enough for the down payment

Paul: No – really?

Jan: Yes. I had enough cash for a down payment, but in those days Jamaica Plain was redlined. You couldn't get a bank loan. Racist as hell. The house was sold to me by the son-in-law of a large Italian family across the street who I liked a lot. Later the mother and I exchanged labor: She looked after my daughter, and I mowed her lawn. I said to the son-in-law, "I can make the down payment, but I don't know how I can get a loan for the rest." He said, "Let me see what I can do."

A few weeks later he came back to me with papers for a loan, which I signed. I stayed up all night the night before I was to sign the deed, because at that time I was in a beautiful apartment in Harvard Square paying $140 a month and didn't know if I could afford the $205 monthly mortgage. I thought, "I'm crazy, I can't do this." I finally did. It was a short loan, 10 or 15 years. I wanted to live at Kenton Road because the neighborhood was a mix of black, brown, Italian, Irish, etc. I was the token hippie. They interviewed me before they would let me live there.

My house was built around 1860 for a farmer and mayor of a part of Boston. He owned several hundred acres of land, and Stonybrook River went through his land. His property consisted of a four-story house and a three-story carriage barn.

The woman next door, who had lived there all her life, told me how the rooms in his house were used. On the ground floor were his kitchen, laundry and dining room. On the main floor were his offices, library and study. The upper floors contained his living quarters. A dumbwaiter connected all of the floors.

I now use the kitchen for a music room, the dining room for my studio, and the main floor for my living area. My kitchen is in his study, and my office is in the barn.

The plaster in the walls is made of a soft material embedded with horsehair, which was typical for that era. That means that the walls have ears, and I often think that all of the conversations over the house's 160 years of existence might have been recorded in the walls, and someday perhaps we will be able to hear them all. They might include conversations from the Civil War period, the War of 1898, World War I and World War II, as well as personal conversations that took place over the years.

What a view that would be of the past history of my house!

Paul: But at the same time, despite all the challenges of dealing with personalities and politics, you were able to do meaningful and productive teaching and research. How did you do that?

Jan: Well, it wasn't easy. Among other challenges, I started the international studios at MIT, but I had a lot of pushback.

Paul: From whom?

Jan: People who said "All the knowledge students need is inside the walls of MIT. You don't have to go outside." I believed differently. I believed it was important to expose students to other cultures.

Paul: Did you have projects in other cultures?

Jan: During that time, I had many projects around the world. So, I knew I could do it, get it started and sustain it. I worked at it and was persistent. We went all over the world. At the same time, John Habraken asked me to design a course for undergraduates' first year, called 401. So, I taught five days a week: three in the studio, and two in the introductory studio.

Paul: So, there were a whole constellation of faculty trying to navigate the same challenges you were, I assume. How did John and others stay above the institutional challenges you were facing?

Jan: John was very much a diplomat. He was able to navigate his way through those challenges. And he was reserved, self-contained. Somehow, he could steer clear of school politics. He was a bit like Andy. Everyone respected John, as did I. The first time I met him we sat and talked at length. I had a tiny office in the main MIT building then. To introduce myself I said, "Here's a project I did in Puerto Rico, which got a PA award, the La Puntilla project." And he said, "You did that?" I said, "Yeah, that's mine." And he said, "That's a project we know in Holland," because it was like what he was doing.

I had a lot of respect for John, and frankly, I think he got tenure for me, because I recall he came to my office late one night and said, "If I were a normal administrator, I would have to tell you that you don't have tenure because half the faculty don't want you to get it. But I am the chair, and I'll get back to you in a day or so." He returned at night and said, "I just want you to know I have supported you for tenure." If it hadn't been for John, I probably wouldn't have gotten tenure and God knows what I'd be doing now.

Paul: I'm sure it'd be something interesting.

Jan: Well, yeah. But sometimes I look back and reflect on my time at MIT — you know, I've taught there for 44 years. Hard for me to believe. And I wonder, what the hell did I do? Let me go back to John's notion of wanting me to start 401. I enjoyed doing that and it was a damn good course for beginning students.

Paul: I do remember it. I remember being aware of it going on when I was a grad student. And then later when I was teaching a revised version of the follow-up course to 404. Tell me more about this unique course. Wasn't there a big model built collectively by all the students?

Jan: Yes. Well, what I did was a series of exercises leading up to the big model. Every week there was an exercise that gave students ammunition, building blocks for how to deal with the final project. The final was a huge site and model which took up three rooms.

Then they were assigned a property, and they had to design a house for a particular client I had established. But they also had to relate their design to their neighbor's site. We had some great final reviews. It was exciting to see.

Paul: Well, you were teaching students how to think about not only their own designs for their parcel, but how their design proposals related to adjacent sites developed by other students simultaneously. You were dealing with the fundamentals of creating community in real time.

Jan: Exactly. So, it wasn't just architecture. It was also how you relate to people. The same thing I'm doing now. That was a good course, and I taught it for many years. At one point I had maybe a half a dozen TAs who had a section, and I gave lectures and did the overall stuff. Sometimes there were over 100 students in the studio.

Paul: Those 44 years, you were teaching hundreds of students and influencing them in ways that are still with them today in the work they do. So you, through your teaching and your love of teaching, love of students, were able to impart knowledge and also share your passion for design. You recognized the power of design and its ability to change people's lives.

Jan: While I was teaching, I would come home and then go into the office in my barn and work until midnight. I've always worked this way. I don't have talent; I have the ability to work. I'm persistent about whatever I do. So that's how the office ran for quite a while. When I was teaching 401, I'd be there in the morning, then I would leave and return in the evening. I was teaching an MIT studio at the same time. When I look back, I am aware that I always felt like an outsider to the department. I never felt engaged in MIT's architecture department as I do now at University of South Florida where I feel very much part of the family of people.

Paul: And why do you think that is?

Jan: Well, at faculty meetings here at USF, people are civil and respectful to each other; willing and inclined to extend genuine praise and goodwill. That was rarely the case at MIT faculty meetings. Often there was chaos and acrimony. At USF there is a different environment.

110 Monticello Ave
Boston, Mass.

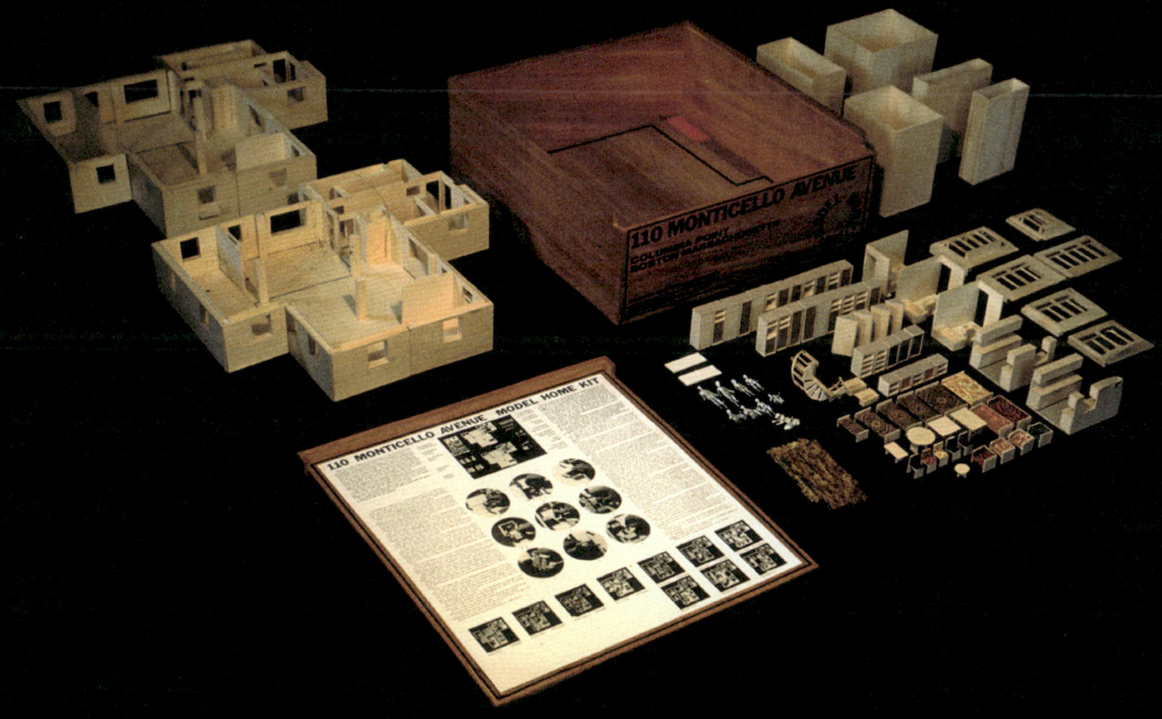

Home model kit

Clients and model of one building

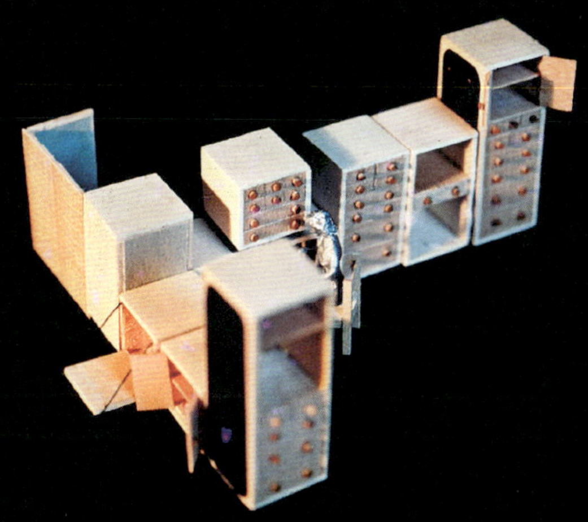

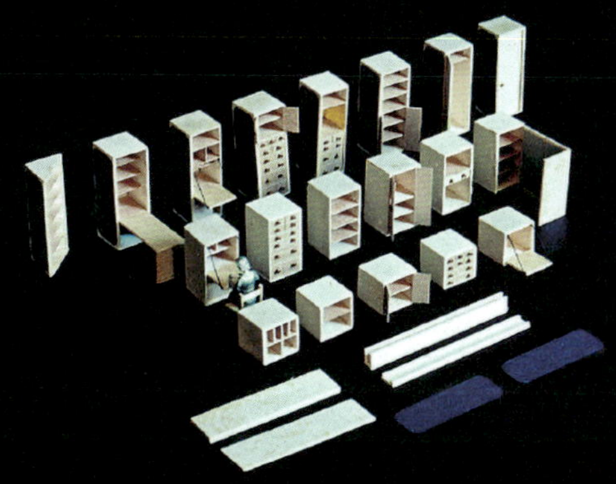

Components of Home model kit and one apartment protype

PART 5

Paul: After receiving tenure at MIT, while still running your office, you learned that you had stage 4 pancreatic cancer. That must have been difficult to go through. How did you navigate this challenge?

Jan: Prior to the diagnosis, I had a plan that, for the first five years I would learn how to practice and what it took to get a building built. I felt I needed to do this from a full-fledged practitioner's perspective, even though, before I was registered or had started the office, I had worked in many offices. I had three sequential five-year plans. In the first five years I would take on any project. I didn't care what it was. I was kind of a family architect, with small projects. I was just learning how to practice. The second five years were for narrowing my focus. And the last five years I would concentrate on a passion, my calling, probably housing. But cancer interrupted my second five-year plan.

During cancer, I had a lot of radiation and chemotherapy. Radiation is one of the scariest things I've gone through. When I started radiation, I would bring a small tape recorder with music, but they told me I couldn't do that because the tape recorder might pick up the radiation. So, I decided that, if I lived six months, I would design a house on a piece of Block Island land I'd gotten in return for a house design. During each radiation treatment I would design a piece of the Block Island house in my head. I never made a sketch. That kept my mind off the horrible Frankenstein machine whirling around me.

When I got a six-month stay of execution, I decided to start building the Block Island house. So, I drew up all the ideas I'd held in my head. On Friday nights after teaching at MIT, I'd drive to the ferry and catch the last boat to Block Island and come back Monday morning. During the weekend I would build. I built everything inside the house. I called it "carpentry therapy," because on Fridays there were faculty meetings which were always difficult, after which I would agonize over what was said, what I should have said, etc. When I had a skill saw in hand, I couldn't think too much about what was going on at MIT, or I'd cut off my finger. Carpentry therapy was a good way to exorcise MIT and do something productive.

The Block Island House took years to finish. Now, decades later, a separate studio building has just been finished.

I couldn't fulfill the last five years of my three-year plan, because of cancer. Cancer forced me to give up projects, because it wasn't fair to clients to keep them in the office. I didn't know if I was going to be around for six weeks or six months, but it wasn't going to be long. Obviously I couldn't take on new work. But I sort of lost momentum during that time. Of course, I practiced afterwards, but it wasn't the same.

And as we've discussed, a lot has changed. Not just the added complexities. Zoom has enabled ways of working all over the world, which weren't possible before.

Later, I had studio projects which enabled students to travel to and design for sites in Cypress, Thailand, China, Costa Rica, Cuba, Ecuador, Chile, Zambia, Turkey, Pakistan, India. There are several projects in Turkey with students, some of which were built. When Bill Mitchell came to MIT as Dean, he brought a strong emphasis on computers. I didn't warm up much to that emphasis, but Bill was a great mind, and his death was a terrible loss.

Jan Wampler Home
Block Island, R. I.

View of Block Island

Views of Block Island

Views of Home in landscape

Sketch model and first drawing

View of Home as part of nature

Home with solar panels

Views at different times of year

Flower gardens

Vegetable gardens

Interior views

Stained glass in windows

Views of studio/gallery building

Turkey Project

Clients and site for Turkey Project

Model of proposed village

View of village

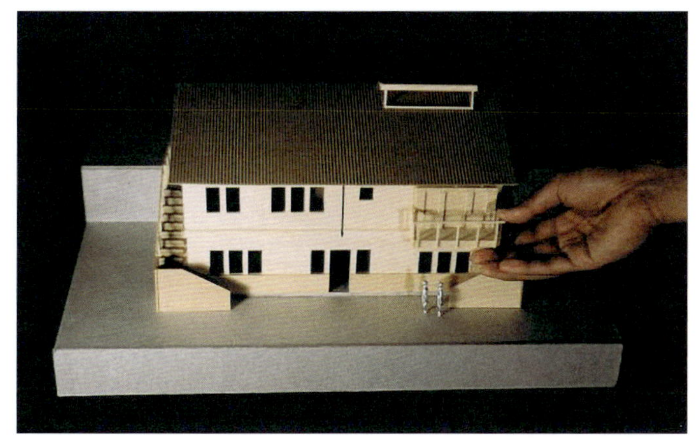

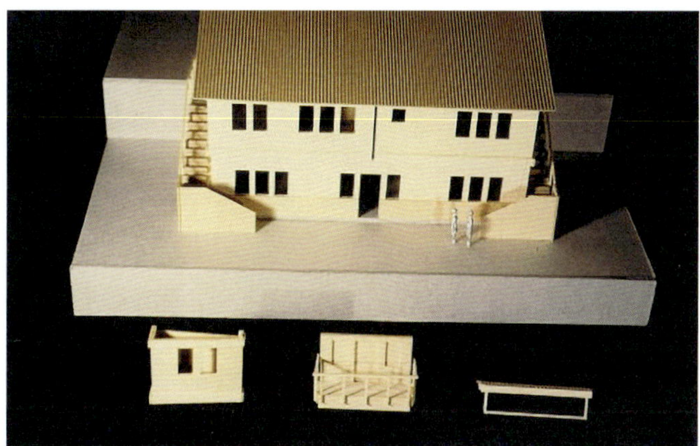

Model of house and variable additions

Sketch model of materials

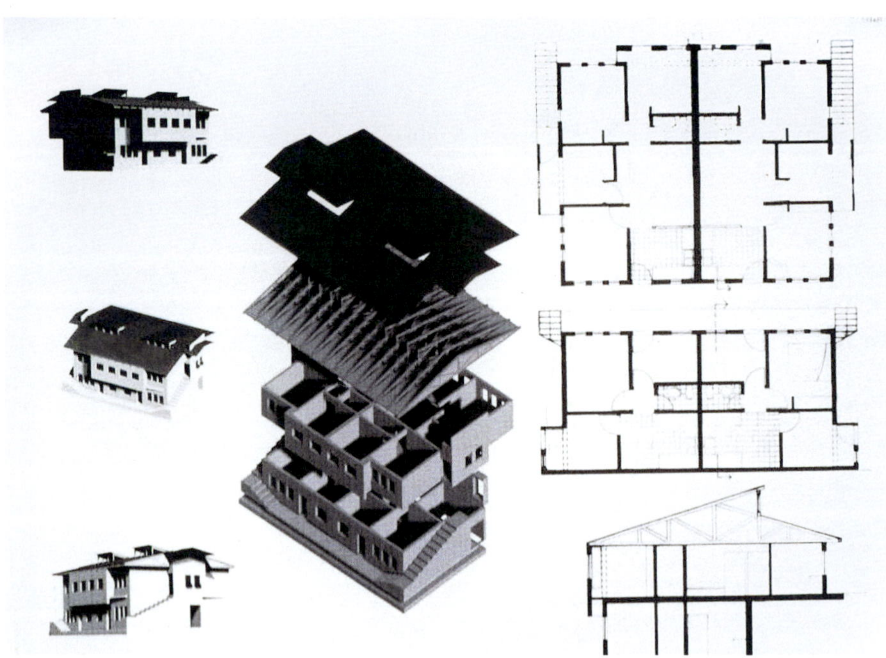

Drawings of typical four-unit house

Model of community center

Final typical house

Buildings under construction

Children of new village

Guayaquil, Ecuador

Near the city of Guayaquil is a large, informal housing project that needed a building to house community facilities. This proposal was created by students enrolled in a workshop in the MIT Department of Architecture. After conversations with the residents of this housing project, a program was established, consisting of a library, spaces for meetings, and a small meeting room. The project was presented to the residents, who then held a party to celebrate the occasion.

Haiti Project, Port au Prince

Haiti has experienced multiple natural disasters in recent years, including hurricanes and earthquakes, which have destroyed many of its buildings. This MIT workshop was asked to design a new village in Haiti, including a school, housing, and community facilities. Designs were made for several housing types, including single, double and multifamily units. Models were made of all of the designs and reviewed by people in Haiti, and hopefully will be built in the near future.

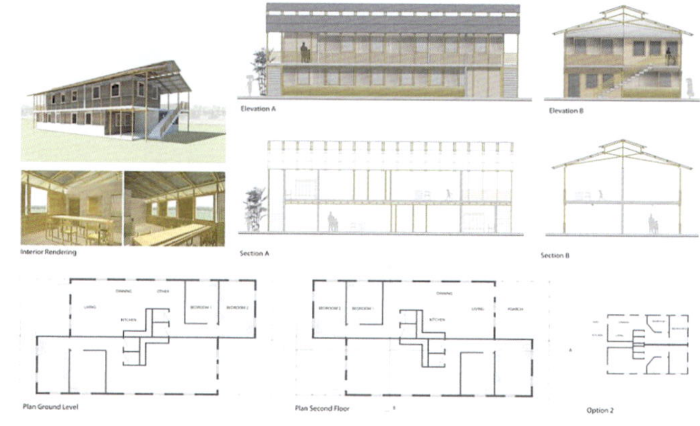

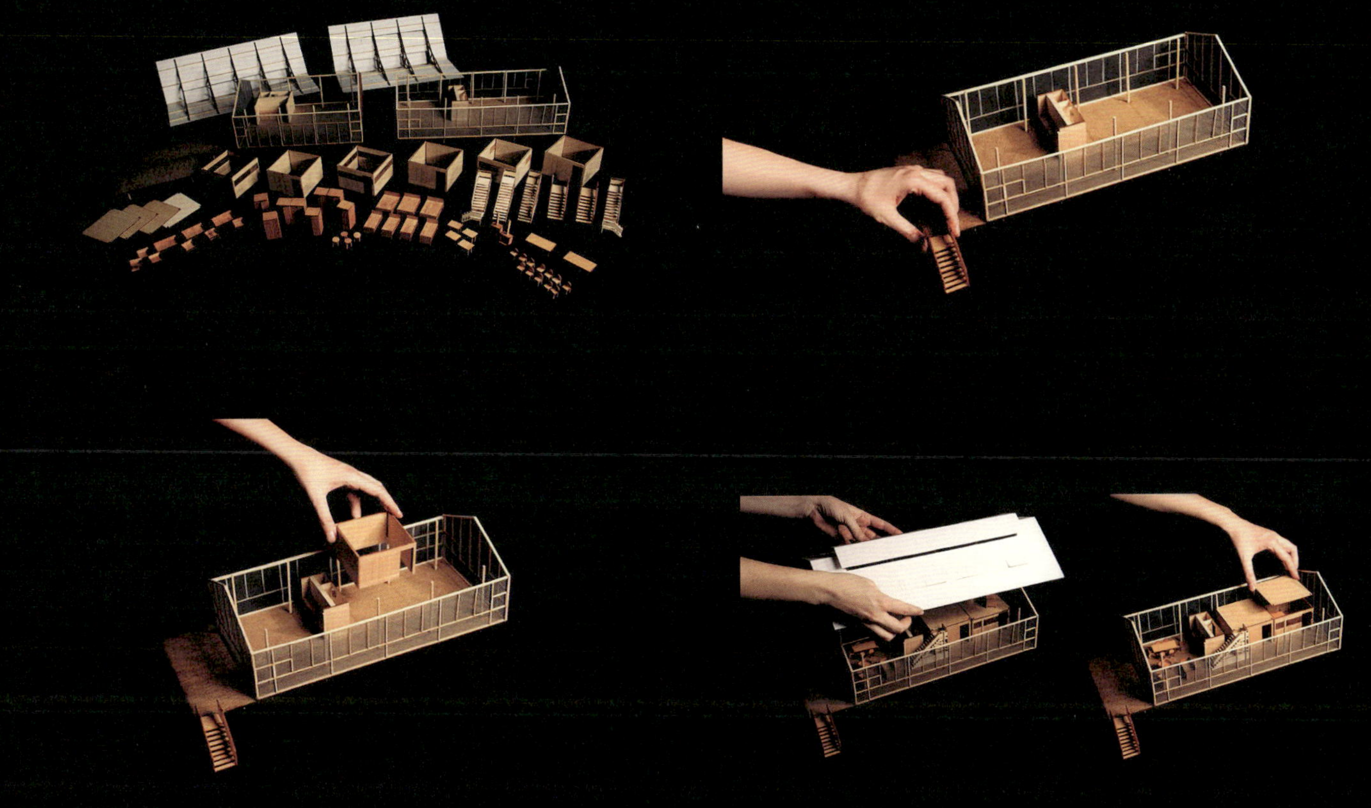

Whale Watch Village, Hawaii

In Hawaii, many young people are interested in farming so their food can be local and not imported. Although Hawaii has had an ideal farming climate and soil for many years, its food has been largely imported. This is about to change.

A local landowner would like to donate land to these young farmers with the goal of helping this endeavor. Her first task was to determine how many farmers could use the land, what facilities were needed for it, and where the new farmers would live. In addition, their houses had to be inexpensive, with the bare minimum of facilities and utilities, which would include water, electricity, bathrooms, cooking facilities, and capacity to add more as economics allowed. A basic design of one large, covered space with enclosing walls was designed and then illustrated with improvements that could be made over the years. In addition, bathing and bath facilities were needed in the farming area.

With the MIT workshop team we tested how long it would take to build one of these buildings. Substantial supplies of bamboo, mud bricks, and cloth were used. We started building in the morning, and by evening the structure was finished.

India Project
Gujarat, India

In Gujarat in Western India, many villages have inadequate housing, consisting solely of ventilation, kitchen facilities, dirt floors, and sunlight. This MIT workshop sent its students to Gujarat to observe the conditions of this housing and to design solutions for it. What was most important about this workshop were our conversations with the residents, who informed us of issues with their housing. From these conversations, we designed ways to improve the housing, which were illustrated in drawings and primarily with a model we presented to the residents. This method was tested with several families. Since the number of presentations was large, we decided to teach only the female participants how to present the project, and they would discuss it with the residents.

in the early morning dawn
before the sun lights the day
I take my tea to the rock
    in the long grass
    waiting for the sun
deer come from the woods
to join me
our eyes meet for a moment
    in the space between

    the long grass dances
    in the morning wind

i watch the house slowly
fill with light of life
    slowly at first
    like a musical score
and understand how the
house
    not only shelters the body
    but the soul

sing house sing I whisper

i reflect on the journey
we are all on
and understand that
what I do
is affected by the journey
through the landscape of life
we are all influenced by
those of the past
    like a train some
    get on before
    some after
    still some after we leave

it is a continuous experience
in harmony with the magic
of the star movements
our thoughts are connected
to others
    no one person can
    remain isolated
    no one country can
    remain isolated
    we are all part of the
    celebration of life

This is the search that all must share
    As the most important search at this
    time.

PART 6

Paul: The profession is changing. My generation, and obviously your generation, probably grew up more in the period when the names of firms were the names of whoever started the firm, whoever put up their shingle. And it was a different concept of design — design as individual versus design as a collaborative. Although there are exceptions, of course, TAC [The Architectural Collaborative] being one of them. I think it's a different generational thing now. Most young people wouldn't want to get started on their own. They would rather do it in a group or partnership, which is a good thing, because it's very hard to do it as a singular entity. I figured this out too late in my career.

Jan: Me too. But part of the issue is the volume of administrative and bureaucratic stuff you must do. Building codes are more stringent than they used to be. So architectural practice is much more complicated and requires a team of people to navigate it. To prepare my students I have them work in teams of three. They're not used to that and it's not easy for them. This semester has been pretty good. There have been no big flare-ups among team members. I say, "Look, no building is ever built by one person. There are consultants, subs and people in the office, so you've got to learn to work on a team." They may not understand this yet, but they might appreciate it someday.

Paul: It seems your concentrated focus on building types has been community housing. Has it been a kind of magnetic north for you?

Jan: It has been. One of the projects I feel good about is the Angela Westover House in Jamaica Plain, which is congregate housing for seniors. I was trying to design a place — I'm doing this again now on Block Island—where residents could enjoy life, look forward to living and not think of as a place they go to die. I worked very hard on that project to try to make a humane environment. I had an excellent client in the Neighborhood Development Cooperation. I enjoyed working with them as they had initiated the idea of a big home, not an institution like most nursing homes at that time.

Paul: I remember seeing photographs of it. I haven't seen it in person. You had hand-drafted tiles embedded in the concrete.

Jan: Twenty-five sunrises. I learned a lot from that experience. I was a tile-cutter for that and would cut the tiles out, put them on a piece of plywood and give it to an old Italian tile-setter, who would set them. One day I handed him the tiles on plywood and went off to get a sandwich. When I came back, he came to me and said apologetically, "I tripped on the steps, so your tile design fell apart. I put them back together the way I thought you might like and hope it is ok." He had to do that because the cement was hardening so he needed to set them. I looked at them and said, "That's great. Why don't you do the next one?" This made it clear that you don't have to do everything on a project. You can provide a framework that others can take and use. I think that's what started the framework for participation that I used on this and other projects. On the opening day, the tile setter brought his children and grandchildren to see his work. He was so proud of it and I was too.

Paul: That's right. You gave him a way of engaging in the design process.

Jan: I went to the Angela Westover House often when I had cancer to have coffee with the workers in the morning to see how it was going and what the problems were. I learned a lot about how to design a place like that, based on what I did but also watching how people used it. I had a bunch of small spots where residents could find privacy, a lot of little outdoor spaces. Two residents met there and married! I thought this was wonderful. I enjoyed that whole process and am very proud of it. And, as you probably know, the project got a design award from the AIA and some other awards.

Paul: That's awesome.

Jan: I don't think much about awards now but at the time, I did, I guess. Of course, I did other projects. Houses and larger projects, like the Haffenreffer Brewery, which was a huge project. I was the architect who started the design for that project. We measured the buildings, about 25 of them, did a basic design for their use and indicated how they could be repurposed. Now it is completely occupied and a wonderful contribution to Jamaica Plain. Mike's Gym, which was an early endeavor, is now a neighborhood highlight, drawing people there.

Paul: Yeah. Really interesting buildings, kind of industrial era. And they were breweries, and now they're turned back into breweries in some cases.

Jan: There were 21 breweries at one time in JP, and they all fed off the Stony Brook River for water. Stony Brook still runs under JP. That's why they located there — because they had a good water source. I visited the Haffenreffer brewery when it was still a brewery, and I remember it well. They had little beer spigots all over the place. Workers would go by and fill up their quart milk bottle with beer and then continue working.

Paul: It makes me think you enjoyed projects that worked with some sort of context or transformation of an existing building, whether it was the Metropolitan Warehouse or a brewery in JP.

Jan: Well, yes. And it's interesting how that's come around again, because people are saying, and rightly so, "Why tear down a building, take it to a dump, and then build something new, when you can rehab?" This saves a tremendous amount of energy and materials. It's happening a lot now and I think it's terrific that we're not always making new buildings. But, yes, a lot of my work was rehab. I don't know if that's because nobody else wanted to do it, or I had good connections and an inclination toward reuse.

Paul: It made for an interesting dialogue between old and new. It relates to the idea of framework. You already had a pre-made framework (i.e., the original building) that you had to contend with through transformation. You layered the old framework with new interventions.

Jan: I also worked in Sienna with ILAUD, the International Lab of Architecture and Urban Design, which was started by Giancarlo De Carlo. Our project was the redesign of the Santa Maria della Scala into an art museum. Santa Maria della Scale was a medieval hospital which had been built over time into an enormous complex of about 40 buildings. Entire streets were enclosed inside. I look back at the list of people who were there. It was an exciting group and a great time. We were there for two months in the summer. Our studios were in the hospital building that we were redesigning. There were people from ten or twelve countries. We would take four to six students with us, and they were embedded in different teams. I would team up with another faculty member to work on the museum design. It was an amazing place.

We worked all day and night, and we lived in Sienna, walked the streets of Sienna. A lot of my ideas about public space came from that experience. I'm still in love with the Compo. I think it's the greatest public space in the world.

Angela Westover House
Boston, Mass.

Sketch model

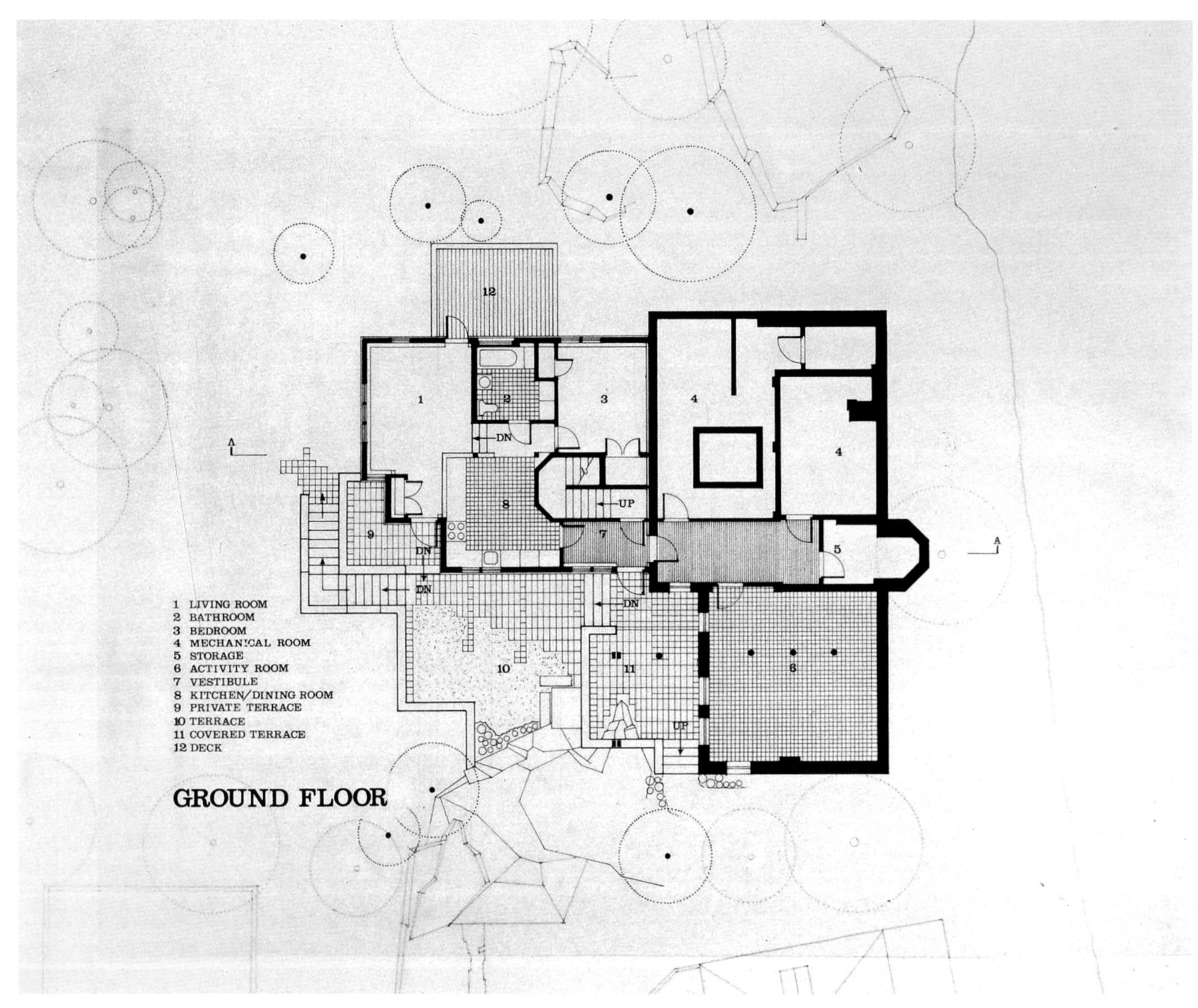

Ground floor plan

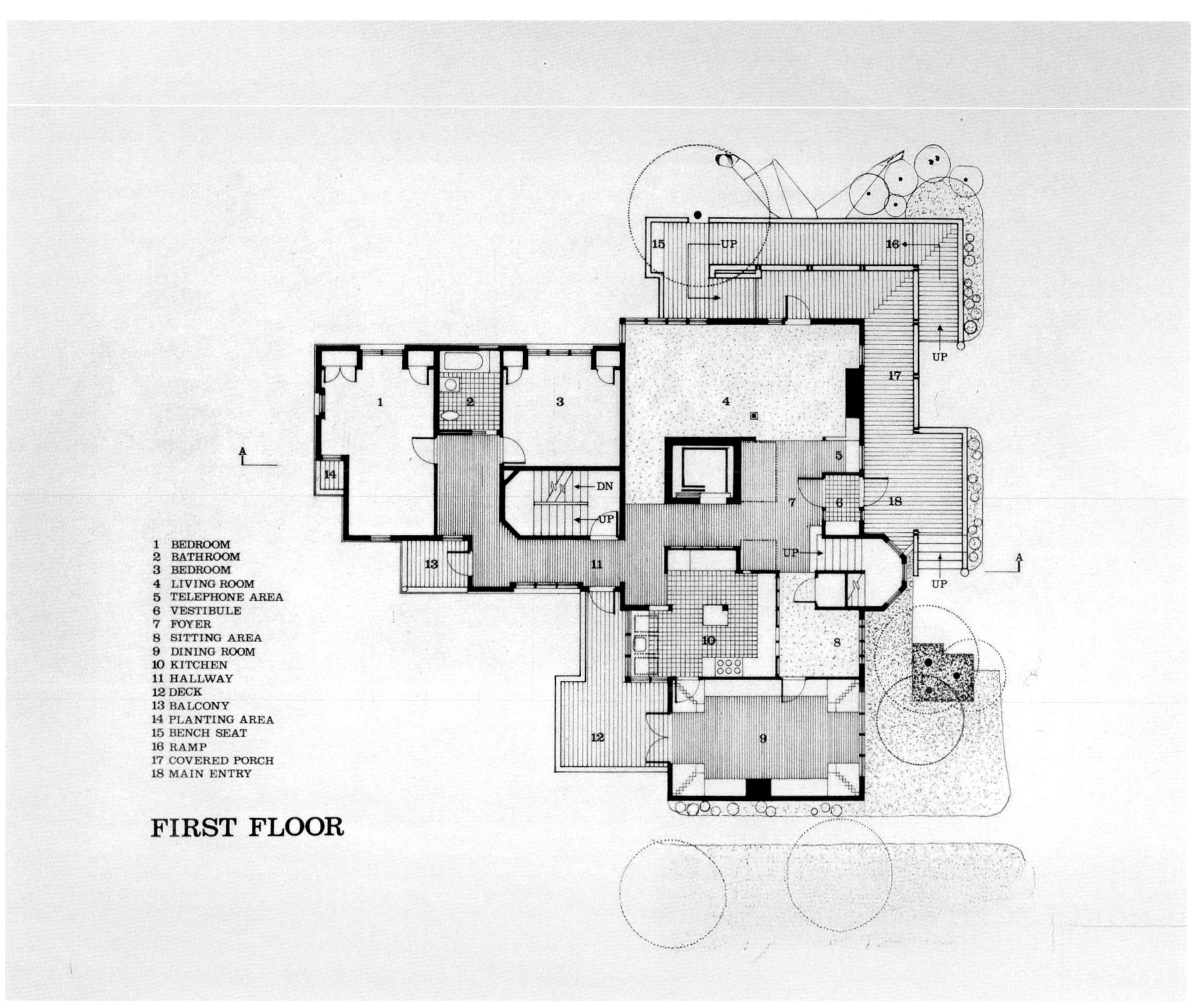

Main floor plan

View of dinning porch

View from street

View of dining room

View of kitchen and dinner cook

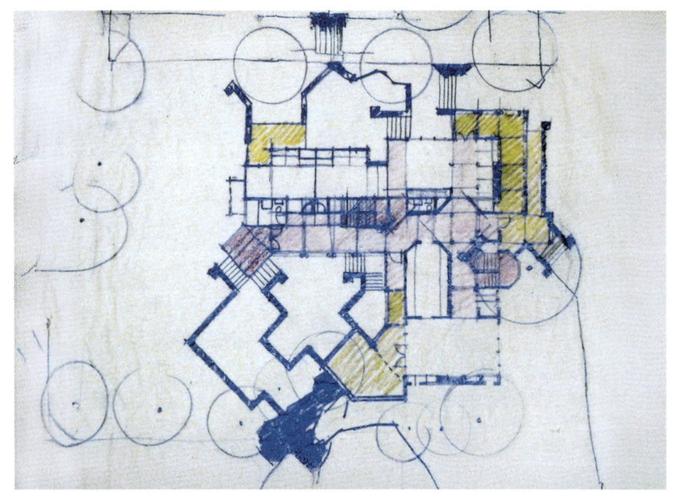
Concept sketch

Construction crew

View from North
Angela Westover House

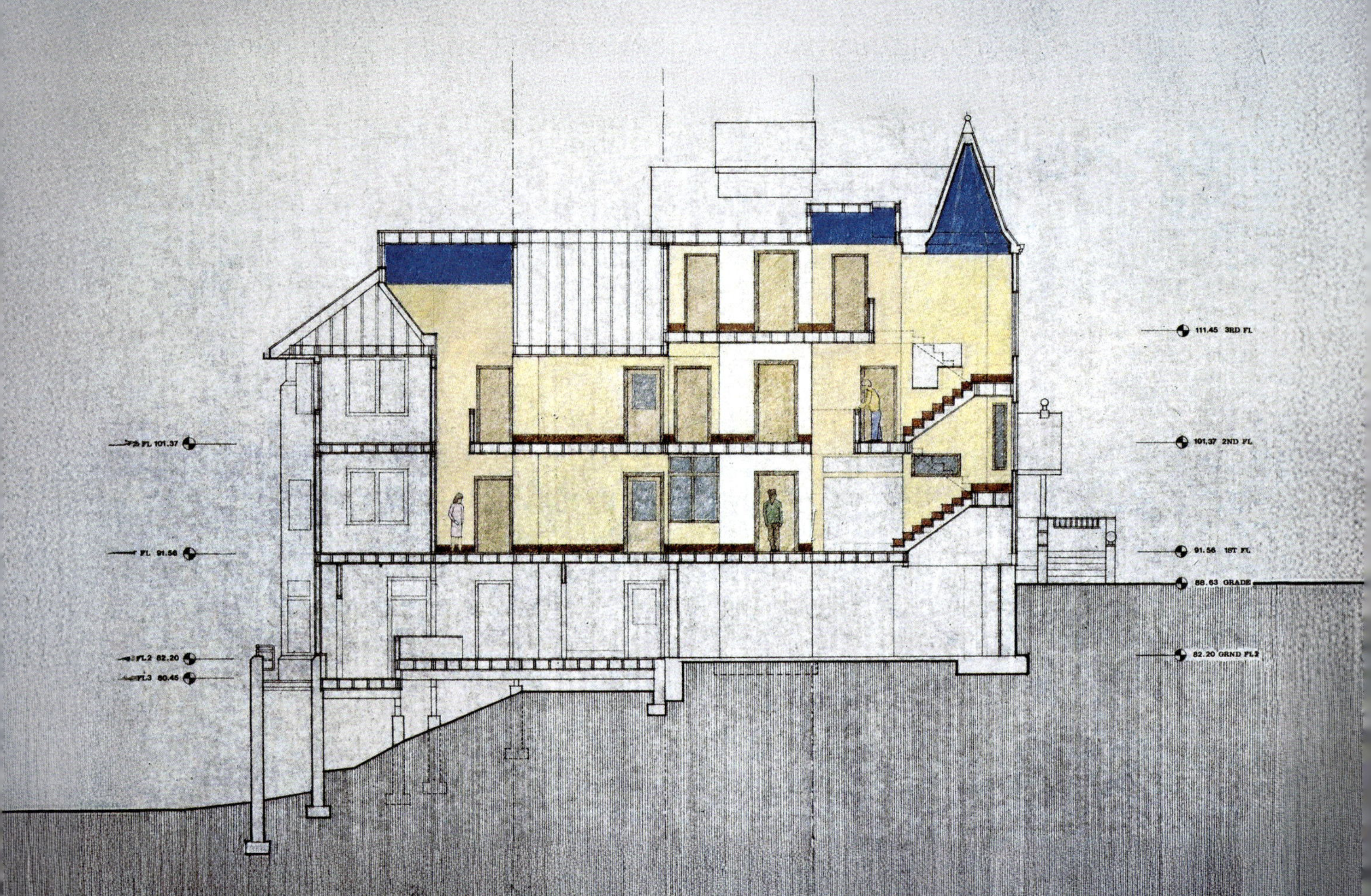

Section through house

Tile at entrance

Sunrise stained glass window

Some of the first residents

Young construction crew made up of artistic craftsmen

Making

i hear the sounds of hammers
and saws
bringing to life
in the morning light
a place for love and companionship

i hear the voices of carpenters
and masons
talking of building a building
to shelter the soul

in the evening sun

Land 1

it starts with the land
    watching it change
    over the year
    watching it grow with no
    help from any person

spring is the most
exciting time
the trees in blossom
all starting at the same time
according to species
a natural response to the sun
    leaves of trees acting
    as solar collectors
    as well as shade from
    the sun

each species finding the
right place to grow

architecture must be the
same
    natural
    adjusting to sky and earth
    changing through the day
    changing through
    the year

can we not make an architecture
that is as beautiful
as a
    spring day
        this we must strive for

Land 2

it starts with the land
    it always has
    the first act is the clearing
    of the land
    to grow food

moving the rocks
    stacking the rocks in
    ordered borders on
    the land
    making divisions
    storing the rocks
    leveling the land ready
    to plant

this is the first act of
architecture
    where it all begins
in any culture at any time
    this has always occurred
    becoming nature and
architecture

the stone borders then can
become walls of
    sheds
    barns
    houses
the walls have openings for
views and ventilation
there is a roof
    like a tree of leaves
a place is made
    from the land and part
    of the land

it is the roots of architecture

Land 3

it starts with the land
    the land gives the clue to
    what is to be designed
    the night before
    a new project
I cannot sleep waiting to see
the land that will guide my
design
when in school I used to take
my sleeping bag and would
camp on the land that had
been given to design a silly
project.
to enjoy the sunset
    the night sounds
    the early morning air
    the smell of the first sun

often I would come back to
school and announce that
this land is too beautiful to
build on and instead should
be preserved for all for years
to come.

and
    I often failed the
    design project.

PART 7

Paul: I thought we could start up where we left off, and that is to talk about your studios, the focus of your international studios that you've conducted at MIT and then later at USF [University of South Florida]. They seem to have played a really important part in how you structure the studio experience and how it frames design problems and speaks of many of the issues that are so important to you, in particular as it relates to having an impact on societal issues. Maybe you can talk a little bit about how you started working on some of your international studios, first at MIT, and how they evolved and developed at MIT and then later at USF, and what you think the impact of those studios has been, both on the students and you as a teacher.

I also know you have been painting. How did that start, and do you enjoy it?

Jan: At MIT I developed ways to expand the typical studio which I felt was too limited in depth, breadth and exposure. I did a lot of different things including designing new courses like 401 which I spoke of earlier and proposing and implementing curricular initiatives. John Habraken was a great support. He gave me a lot of latitude. Later I was asked to lead the Undergraduate Design Program which I redesigned, adding studios to give students more design opportunities, incorporating an undergraduate thesis, and staging exhibitions of their work. One outcome was that students emerged with a stronger portfolio to show prospective employers and use in graduate school applications.

For much of my adult life I've been aware of the huge number of people in the world who do not have adequate housing. I saw this firsthand wherever I went. In the early days of China, way back when I first went there to teach, there were no high-rises in Beijing and then they developed like wildfire. What upset me most was that they were all copycat American ideas. I would bring magazines and they'd look at the cover photo and say, "We like this one." And they would replicate it.

I was concerned that the United States was mucking up the world by superimposing what we considered good architecture on other cultures. My international studios were intended to prepare students to design for cultures with different needs and opportunities. Also, the international experiences made me aware of how widespread and urgent the need for adequate housing was. The premise of the international studios was simple: take students to other cultures, expose them to how people lived there, and design a final project so when these future architects and planners practiced, they would know better than to superimpose the American way.

I started taking students all over the world — China, India, Pakistan, Turkey, Zambia, several South American and Central American countries — and had projects in each location. I wouldn't go unless the government or an interested group there invited me. Also, I would only go if I had a group of clients whom my students could speak to. Those groups were typically NGOs [non-governmental organizations]. The students also interacted with people who lived in the shacks near our site. I insisted on having a group the students could relate to. I was surprised at how much they valued these experiences.

We went to Turkey and talked to the people after the first earthquake. We've been to Turkey to do projects there many times since. But the first time I went with students, we talked with people who were living in tents, and heard from them what they wanted from a new house. Their input served as our criteria for the project. We also introduced students to the area's vernaculars and local materials. We visited old Istanbul and villages and learned how they were built. So, students got a first-hand education about other places through direct contact and immersion. They usually came back with a different attitude about architecture than what they had before. Then we built. Not all the time, but we built quite a few things.

Paul: What type of building would you build?

Jan: We did a community center in Costa Rica. We designed and built a playground area. In India, a model house for how to improve ventilation and heat. I learned that respiratory disease of babies is very high in those countries because they're on the floor, and the fires for cooking and heating are on the floor. We worked in Pakistan to develop a new stove that was off the floor.

Paul: Wonderful.

Jan: We did a lot of different things. I had an international studio every semester for 20 or 25 years.

Paul: That is quite an accomplishment!

Jan: MIT has come a long way from the designs that were produced when I first got there, compared to what it is now. Moving on, when I left MIT — I went to Florida, not thinking about teaching — I had a client who wanted me to design a house in Gulfport on the west coast of Florida, so I went to look at the site. That was how I found the town. The house was never designed or built. It was 2007 at the start of a major recession. But this introduced me to Gulfport, and I fell in love with the town.

Paul: It's easy to do.

Jan: It's a quaint little place. And still interesting and distinctive though it's becoming too discovered, so to speak. It has a strong gay community and vibrant artistic vibe.

While I was there the wife of a University of South Florida faculty member who somehow knew I was in Florida contacted me. She had been my student in China. We went to dinner one night and they said, "You should drop by USF and see what they're doing, and maybe you might teach there." I said, "I'm not really interested in teaching right now but, yeah, I'll come by." So, I did and was so impressed with the students in Steve Cook's class when he was teaching the Core Studio. Students were building models and doing drawings, in contrast to MIT where students worked mostly on computers, making it hard to fully get what they were doing.

By coincidence, the Director of the USF School of Architecture and Urban Design was Robert MacLeod who had heard about me from students when he attended Harvard GSD years earlier. Back then, Bob wanted to take my studio but couldn't arrange it within the GSD curriculum. Bob got his first degree at University of Florida, Gainesville, and taught there. UF grads who applied to MIT were strong candidates with impressive portfolios and model building skills. At the end of my visit to USF I left my name and CV at his office "just in case", thinking, "Well, that's that." Then one day I called Bob, and he offered me a job.

Paul: That's great.

Jan: I said, "Well, all right, I'll do it for a semester on the condition that I can teach a studio similar to what I have done in

MIT workshops." The workshops had that approach where we traveled to experience the site firsthand and talked to people who lived there. There have been exceptions, due to circumstance. For example, Ukraine is an exception because we can't go there now and there were exceptions due to COVID travel restrictions. That was unfortunate. But like with Ukraine I found clients who designed houses who were from Ukraine. With USF students we have traveled to Cuba, Chile, Ecuador, Cyprus, Thailand, and Puerto Rico. I think it's great that USF's architecture program incorporates travel which gets students out of Florida.

Paul: So, you took your students to Barcelona this last year.

Jan: Yes, I did. Regrettably not many could go because they couldn't afford it, and some had visa problems. But those who did had a great experience

Paul: Well, how were the studios funded? Were they funded by the universities, or by outside donors?

Jan: In the beginning I had some funds from people who gave me money. Not a lot, but enough to enable students to travel. But at USF, the idea is that the students pay their own way.

Paul: So, all the trips that you took with the students at USF were paid for by the students?

Jan: Except for the ones for which I could find funding.

Paul: That must be difficult, because a lot of the students don't necessarily come from families with a lot of resources.

Jan: Some of them have two jobs to help pay for their education and other expenses. One worked at Home Depot, one worked as a waiter, another worked at the school. They had all kinds of different jobs. Some were married. Somehow, they have found time to work. They're very dedicated and hardworking.

Especially in later years some of my MIT students were a little entitled, and wealthy. I would take students on the semester's first field trip to see the site and I'd say, "We'll meet in front of 77 Mass Avenue, and I need two more cars besides mine, to drive everyone." I'd park there, look for the other cars and, not finding what I expected as student-driven vehicles, go look for them. More than once, I found a student driving a Mercedes. It blew me away!

Toward the end of teaching at MIT, I had a student who was having problems working. I took her aside, and said, "You're just not producing enough or working enough, not by anyone's standards, let alone mine." She said, "Oh, I thought all I had to do was to get into MIT. I didn't know I had to work once I got here." She was very honest and naïve. I found it humorous, in a way. I haven't had USF students like that. They tend to be industrious. They expect to work hard. They have jobs. They don't come from privileged backgrounds. I always paid for my TAs and myself and my own travel, etc. because it seemed wrong to have students pay.

I think USF's program is great in getting students out there to see other things.

This year they traveled quite a bit. We went to Barcelona, an interesting city — not only because of Gaudi's work, but the character of the city. The students hadn't traveled for two or three years due to COVID, so they wanted to go somewhere.

My studios all reflect my belief that large cities are becoming a thing of the past and villages are our future. Already many people have moved or are moving to small towns and villages. The reasons include affordability, better educational options for children, richer social life, and tighter-knit communities. Also, technology enables working from home at least part of the time. I believe village life is the direction of the future. That's why most of my studios have been about designing a new village which is as self-sufficient as possible.

Paul: Such as in Ukraine.

Jan: Yes, Ukraine is an example. I tell students that the "what" of architecture is important. We must design beautiful buildings. That's what we do. But we also must design with sensitivity to the “whys,” that is, to address the content, the program. So, I have students develop a “why” for what they’re doing that considers potential best use, higher purpose, and then to support it, work it out. Some of the ideas are a little off the wall but that’s okay.

Paul: You’re upset that most buildings are not about the “why”?

Jan: I am upset that most of the buildings we must do in practice are not about the “why” of the buildings. They’re what somebody else thinks they should be. I don’t believe that somebody else has a better sense of the “why” than we architects do. So that was always a consideration in my studios. It seems like a fundamental issue — what is the “why” of what we do as architects, and how does it relate to our service to society? The “why” establishes our trajectory as a profession. If we don’t pose and answer that question, then we’re in trouble. Anything can happen.

Paul: And anything goes.

Jan: You’re doing some wonderful work with sustainable issues. This must be a major consideration. Unfortunately, a lot of the buildings one sees may be well-designed but many of the solutions are superficial; they only brush the surface. I don’t want to pick on anybody, but there are architects whose main goal seems to be to make a monument to them-self. They get a lot of attention.

On the other end of the spectrum, a woman in India was just recognized for her work to help residents in vulnerable communities. I remember distinctly, when I was in India, with a well-known architect there, I asked him about the larger issues of housing for so many poor people. His answer was that the issue is too large to do anything. I found his response very disappointing. I think this is the most important issue for the future.

Paul: Well, I wonder if his intentions were molded by the experience of living in India at that time, and recognizing that the problems were so overwhelming that, in a situation like that, there are just limits to what people in the profession can do. The solutions might require people and institutions outside the frame of reference that we typically deal with.

Jan: That’s right. But our profession has not paid enough attention to models in other realms where important work is being done that truly serves humanity. Doctors Without Borders is an example. That organization, founded by doctors and journalists, has been so effective in serving and saving people around the world. I wish there were an Architects Without Borders or something like that. Using a similar model, architects would be ideally suited to address the worldwide shelter crisis effectively and humanely.

There’s no question that the need is acute. The problems are ten times worse than in 1948 when Eleanor Roosevelt addressed the United Nations in a Universal Declaration of Human Rights asserting the need for adequate housing as a basic human right. There are now two billion people, 20% of the world’s population, who don’t have it. And that number is increasing.

Paul: And the impact is going to be even more pronounced, given the demands and challenges of climate change, which particularly impact people of lesser resources.

Jan: Our next big challenge is access to water. We’re running out of fresh, safely managed drinking water. We must figure out ways to deal with that. We see the migration problem of Central America coming already in the United States, I don’t think it’s anything compared to what’s going to happen when people don’t have water. Currently many don’t have food, and that’s bad enough. You can go longer without food than you can without water. The problem will get worse.

Paul: Well, it’s going to be a huge problem in the United States. I mean, look what’s happening with the Colorado River.

Jan: Exactly.

Paul: And even in places like California where they’re without water, they have [had] a drought for several years, then suddenly, they have a year where the soil can't absorb all the water. You get these massive runoffs.

Jan: Not only that, but I have seen the Colorado River when it reaches Mexico. It's a dirty stream about ten feet wide or less, because we have used all the water.

Paul: To end this section, I know you have been painting. Can you talk about how this started, and are you enjoying doing it?

Jan: Yes, I started about three years ago. I had not painted since RISD, where I did paint, as well as working in other disciplines.

I enjoy painting immensely. It's very relaxing and enjoyable. With architecture, you must wait at least three years to see how the building turned out and if you like it. But with painting, with watercolors, you know within three minutes if it is good or bad. That can be rewarding. Of course, I throw away more than I keep.

I use Chinese watercolors on Chinese rice paper and have learned a lot from studying Chinese paintings. There is a simple magic to them. I bring back from China materials to work with. Mostly I paint what I call "Sun Shadows" and have had several openings, on Block Island and in Gulfport. I find it exciting to see them in an exhibition and think about how I can improve them.

I say, "Old architects don't die; they just paint away."

Paintings

Distant Sky 1
16" x 18" Watercolor on rice pape

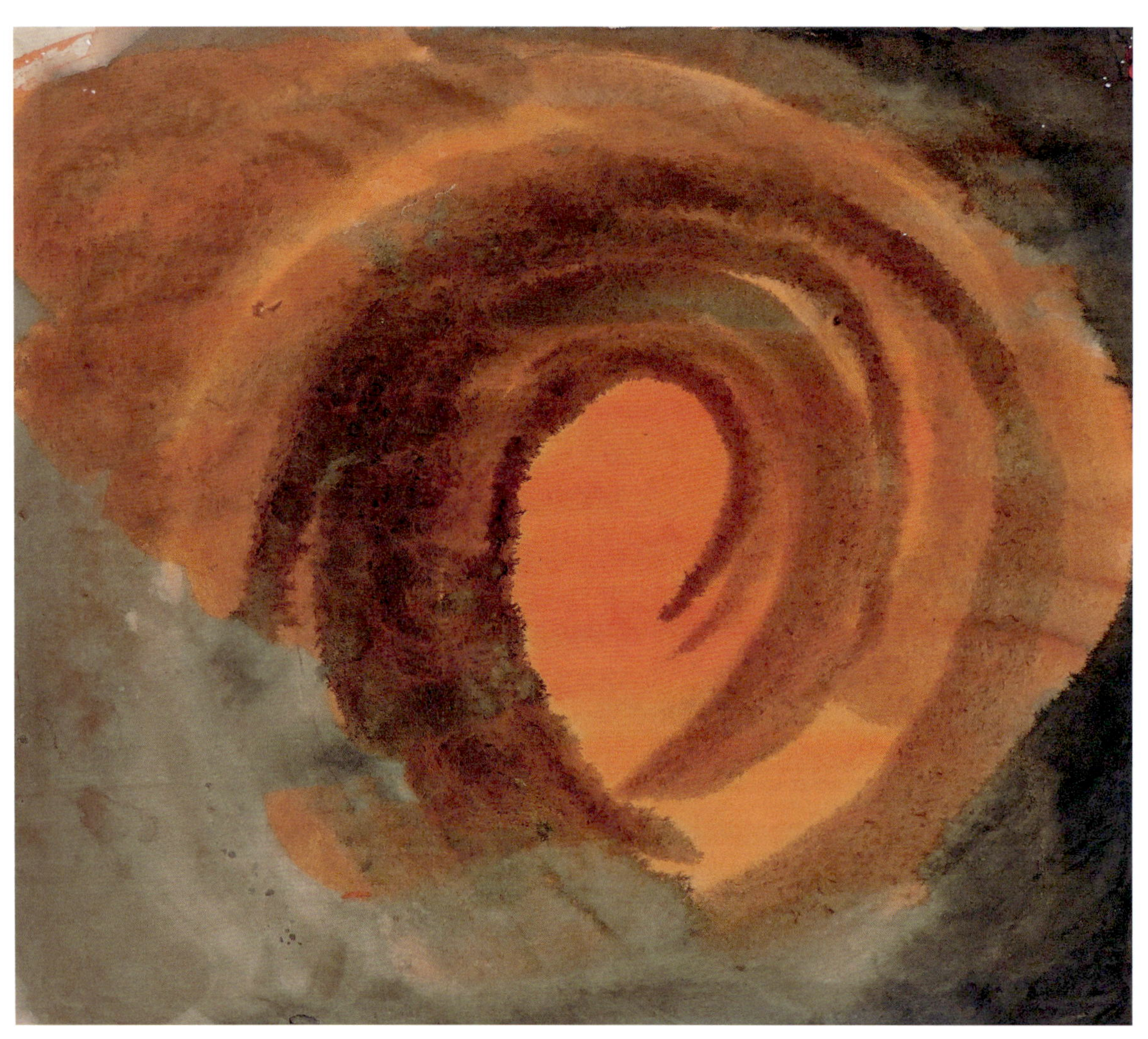

Distant Sky 4
14" x 16" Watercolor on rice paper

Sky Shadow 6
12" x 18" Watercolor/ink on rice paper

Distant Sky 8
14" x 20" Watercolor/ink on rice paper

Abstract 7
20"x 20" Watercolor on rice paper

Distant Sky 9
14" x 14" Watercolor on rice paper

Sky Shadow 7
14" x 20" Watercolor on rice paper

Sunset 9
16" x 20" Watercolor/ink on rice paper

Abstract 11
16" x 16" Watercolor on rice paper

Sky Shadow 9
14" x 16" Watercolor on rice paper

PART 8

Paul: I think it ties to the previous conversation talking about the "why" of architecture. I think the "why" of Jan Wampler has always been there. It's been very consistent.

Jan: Well, yes, perhaps so. Again, I was raised on a farm, a poor farm that had food, but no money. I think that has stuck with me. So, frankly, I always feel at home when I go into a squatter slum. Somehow those people seem like kindred spirits.

Paul: So, you were still affected, I assume, by the generation of people who took on the Depression head-on, that that ethos still was part of the culture. And it was one that focused also on the role of community versus the individual, because it was impossible to survive without the support of the community, from what I have read and heard from my elders, my grandparents and others of that generation.

Jan: Absolutely. My grandfather on my father's side was the head of something called Prairie Radicals in Ohio. Prairie Radicals believed that, because of the Depression, as you said, the only answer was a cooperative way of looking at issues. At the same time, expensive farm machinery was coming in, which local small farmers couldn't afford. They said unless we organize as a community, we'll be wiped out by big business. Which is, of course, what happened. Many small farms have been replaced by huge farms. Growing up on the family farm, I was not aware of my background and what it meant, but perhaps it comes with my DNA.

Paul: It's part of your DNA. But it's also, if you combine the circumstances, the location, and the culture of what the United States was — in particular, Ohio — at that time when you were growing up, it all makes sense, I think, in retrospect. So going back to the idea of the "why" of Jan Wampler, there's a consistency there, but it was fed and nurtured by the people who were in your life and the people you encountered as your career evolved.

Jan: Yes. But I don't think I ever knew it.

Paul: No, of course not. It's something that maybe becomes more visible and decipherable over time as you get to reflect on your career, and who you are as a person over time, as dictated by all these circumstances.

Jan: I was very fortunate to be in that situation. I didn't know it at the time. I was just doing what I thought I should be doing.

Paul: In thinking about the impact of USF Studios and MIT Studios, you've also touched upon the future of architecture, and implications of what its role might be, if not through implication, through the direct examples. But I wonder if you could give some advice to the students of the future, given this important moment in our history, both as a country and as a culture, and certainly as an architectural community. What type of advice would you offer young students or aspiring students of architecture?

Jan: A few pieces of advice. The first is that you must be passionately involved with what you're doing when you design. It's not a job. It's a dedication to something that inspires and guides how you focus your life.

Paul: Vocation, maybe.

Jan: Exactly. When I go to bed, I'm still designing the project I'm working on. To repeat: it's become much harder to get something built now. If you are not dedicated to what you're doing, then it's just a job and a laborious one, at that. You must believe in and be passionate about what you are doing. At times, anything that can go wrong will go wrong. Things you never imagined. If you aren't passionate about architecture — to some extent, driven — you may as well be in some less demanding profession because you won't have the persistence and commitment to hang in there. Sometimes students ask in studio "Do you think what I'm doing is right?" And I say, "Well, do you think what you're doing is right? That's more important than what I think."

I know that absorption in career and work is not popular right now; work is not as central to people's lives as it once was. Since COVID people are less inclined to work as much and as hard. A career is not as high a priority. Many people put in 35 hours a week, and that's it. That isn't how architecture works. Sometimes you must work all night to meet a deadline.

Paul: Yeah. The culture has definitely changed. I think part of it is the computer.

Jan: Yes.

Paul: Because the one thing about the computer is, it requires and absorbs all your concentration and focus. Working in a group setting, in a studio is different, where you're feeding off others. Here, you're just looking at a machine, and the machine is talking to you, and you're responding. Consequently, it's very demanding. And so, the 40 hour-a-week experience working with a computer is a very stressful, very different experience than 40 hours working as part of a design community.

That said, computers and software are developing new ways in which we can collaborate in real time across geo-spatial domains, offering us entirely new ways of designing.

Jan: COVID made it worse. At USF, the consensus is that it will take us two years to recover in terms of teaching. Students still want to work at home on their computers, as they did from 2020 to 2022. Not in the studio.

Paul: Maybe students will want to be together more in the future.

Jan: I hope so. This is about passion too. Another piece of advice I've spoken of is that we must design the most beautiful buildings we can. However, we must also design buildings that relate to culture, clients, site, materials and needs of society, and make something beautiful within that framework. Because as I've said, we are the primary custodians of the physical/built world. And we're creative, visionary, intelligent, able and inclined to make beautiful things with limited resources. I find it more interesting when I have a narrow set of parameters within which to work.

I had a client on Martha's Vineyard who gave me no direction whatsoever and no budget limitation. I was paralyzed. It was hard to get started. For example, when there's only one window type I can use to stay within budget, I must be creative in finding how many ways I can use it. I think limitations are good. This applies to designing shelter for two billion unhoused people around the world, considering environmental conditions, limited resources, etc. This is the new generation's challenge, what they must think about. Not how to be on the cover of a magazine — though maybe they will be on the cover. This is one of the reasons I admire your work Paul: the beautiful house you designed addresses sustainable issues, both practically and elegantly.

Paul: Oh, thank you.

Jan: We must make beautiful architecture. Education is important in preparing people to do this. I'm critical of education. Too often assignments at the GSD and RISD were to design homes for millionaires or do other designs for privileged people. That's not what I think we should be doing. Education needs to focus students on the important issues too. That's where students learn and where they formulate values; it's from the teaching. So, I'm critical of our profession and our educational direction. But I'm also very hopeful. This is reflected in the architect's oath I wrote in 2022 which is now part of USF's graduation ceremony and is being used on other campuses.

The younger generation is very motivated to tackle the issues of climate change. One reason, of course, is existential. But also, they understand the damage we have done and are doing to the earth and what we stand to lose, in ways that earlier generations including ours haven't fully grasped.

The oath I wrote was not easy to get approved by my peers. I encountered strong resistance within my profession. In the process of writing it, I went through 20 different versions. Throughout it all I maintained that architects must acknowledge and address climate change. There was huge pushback from the profession on that point. They said it was "too political." When I presented the oath to USF students, I asked for their feedback. They said unequivocally that if I had not included climate change, they would not take the oath. That was exciting to me and affirmed my faith in the next generation.

Paul: Maybe we could finish up with two questions. One is, which work that you've done are you most proud of? You already talked about your next project in Turkey, and the anticipation of doing that. Could you answer those questions in the next couple of minutes?

Jan: I think the project that I'm most proud of will be my next one. I just finished a design for Block Island which I'm excited about. It combines a library and senior housing. Local politics can make Block Island a tough place to work. We'll see what happens. Obviously, this project is not built yet. If that is to happen it will take a long time. I'm always excited about the next project, whatever it is.

In terms of past projects, I've done work I've forgotten about until someone reminds me of it. I got an email last week from someone whose apartment I'd apparently redesigned. They showed me images and it wasn't bad, but I don't remember it. My office was interrupted when I got cancer, but I did a lot of work before that in my community here and other places. I have no idea how many buildings I've built. I've never counted.

I feel very close to the Angela Westover House, because it was about the "why." We broke ground on that project not only architecturally, but also in terms of what housing for older people could be. I feel good about that. And I got several awards for it. The awards themselves don't mean much but recognition for the approach and outcome does.

So that's a good one. And there's a little house in Maine that I designed for a man and woman who retired. He was a professor at City College in New York who wanted to spend the rest of his life praying for peace. She was a marriage counselor who wanted to spend the rest of her life making collages. It was a struggle to build their house, but it turned out well. I haven't seen it for years. The client used to call and say, "I want you to know I'm sitting here in the sun, looking out over the snow. I want to thank you for designing such a beautiful place for us." That means much more than an award.

I'm sure there are others. For a long time, when I did a rehab or designed a new home, I would make a piece of stained glass as a housewarming gift. For the house in Maine, I made several. I usually take three years to build a house so making a piece of stained glass is much more immediate. You cut your fingers and struggle with the glass. It is different than the house design.

Also very meaningful to me is a project I am working on now, related to Eleanor Roosevelt's advocacy for adequate housing in the "Universal Declaration of Human Rights," 75 years ago.

There are 200 countries representing the United Nations that need adequate housing. There are also about 200 schools of architecture in North and South America. I propose that each school select ten students. We assign a UN country to each of them, as their client. Information is provided about that country's climate, local materials, and geographic conditions. Using this information, the students design a home for their client.

It could be done as a short sketch project with outcomes including a model, plans, views, user perspective and basic building information. Awards would be given for the best designs. Then recipients would team up with a practicing architect and with their client to get the design built. The final projects could be exhibited at the United Nations.

The intention is to build houses that demonstrate simple solutions to problems, and to lead to aspirations and solutions for larger scale problems like providing schools and health facilities. Because when someone has a home of their own, they are more likely to aspire to more.

This project could produce housing prototypes quickly and affordably, raise funds to build them and be a bold mission-driven effort led by architects.

I don't know if that answers the question you asked.

Paul: It's a great answer, and it's a good way to finish up as a reflection on all your contributions and the role that giving has played in the act of describing who you are as a person and as an architect and addressing this issue. How your work has exemplified so many positive ways to contribute to people's lives in society at large.

On behalf of all those hundreds of students you taught over the years, thank you for sharing so much of yourself in these pages and throughout your career.

So thank you, Jan.

Jan: Thank you. Let's end where we began, with Walt Whitman. Some words of his to which I relate: "When once I am convinced, I never let go."

Chandler Home
Maine

View of ocean through curtain of trees

View of ledge in center of site

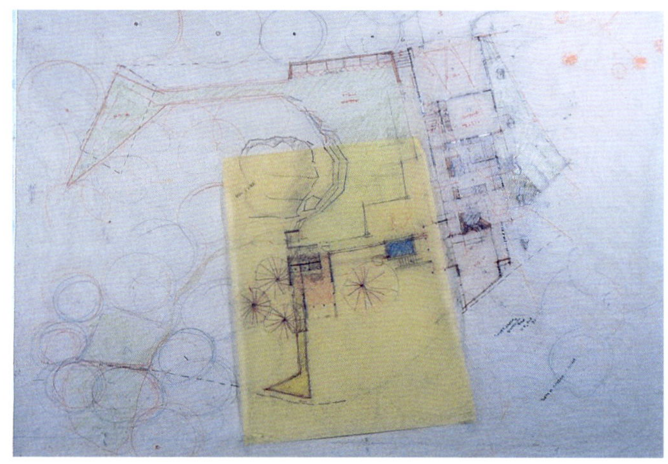

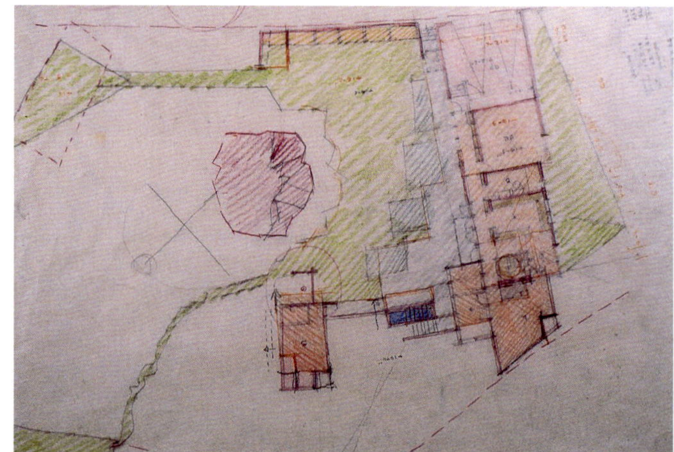

Sketch design with ledge in center

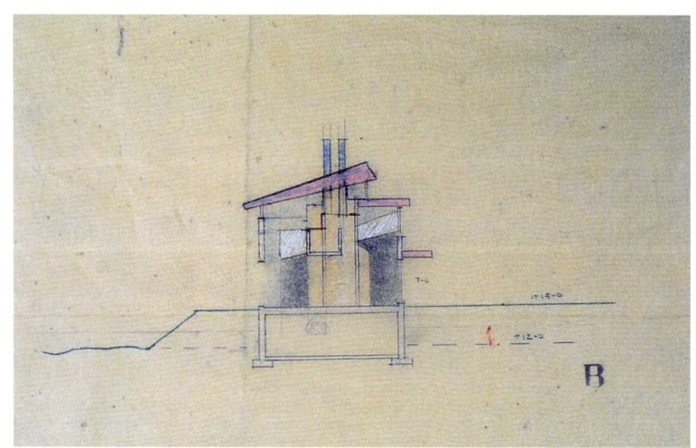

Sketch showing two story space

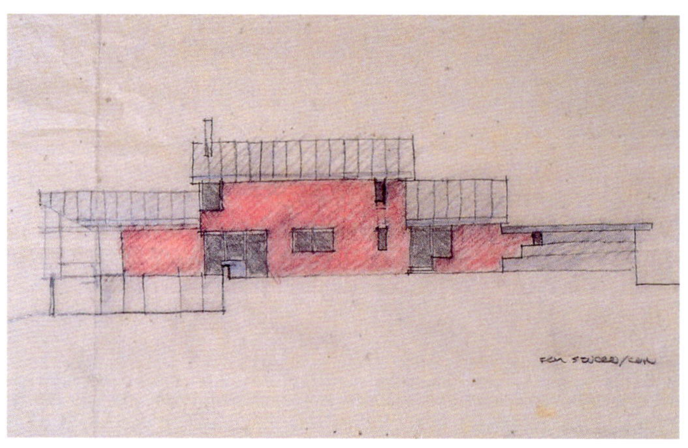

Sketch of North Elevation

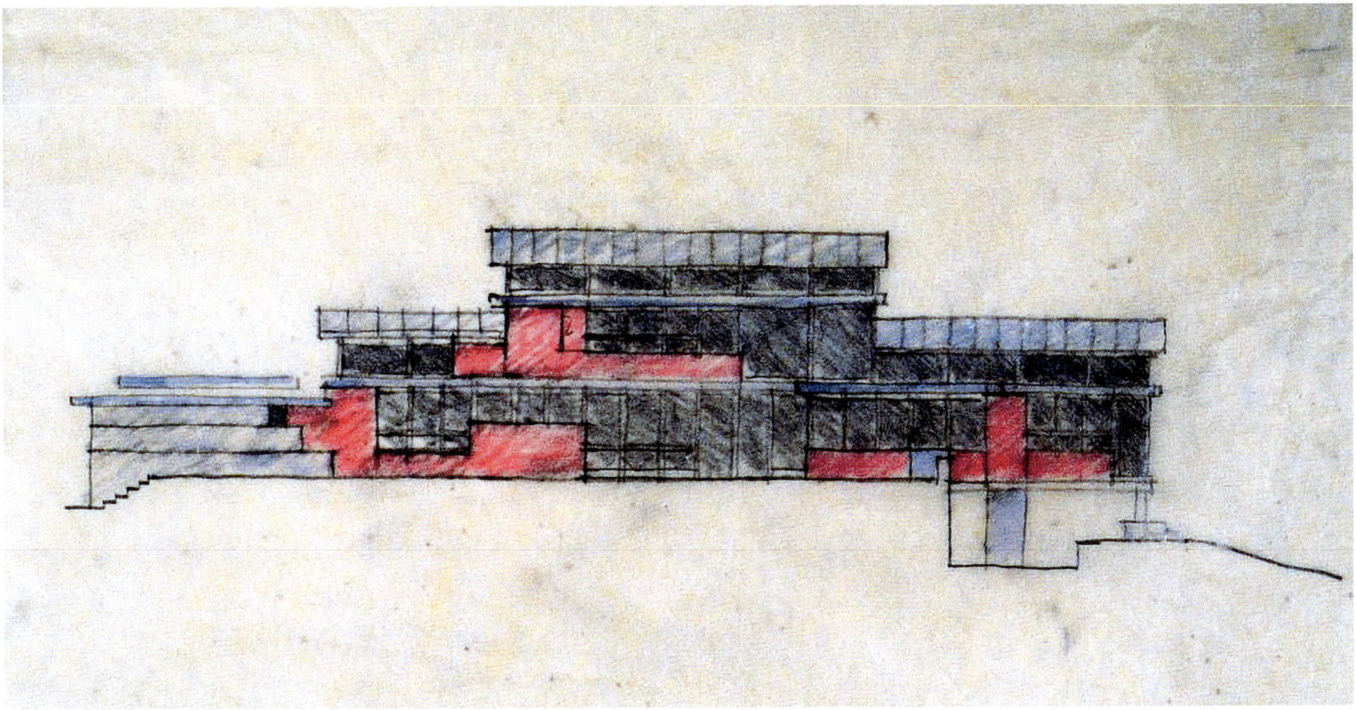

Sketch of South Elevation

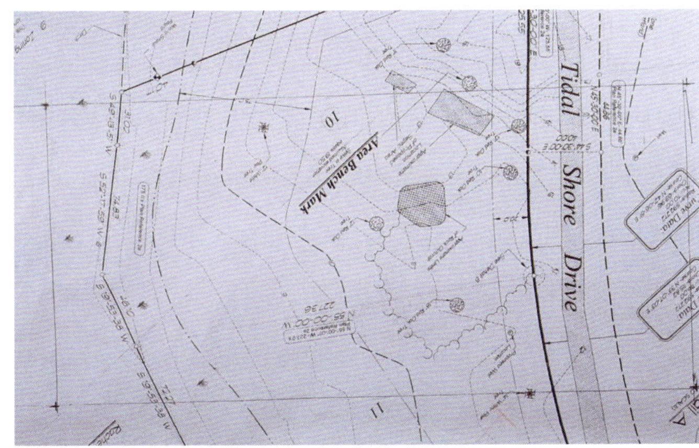

Site Survey with setback line on left

First sketch of design

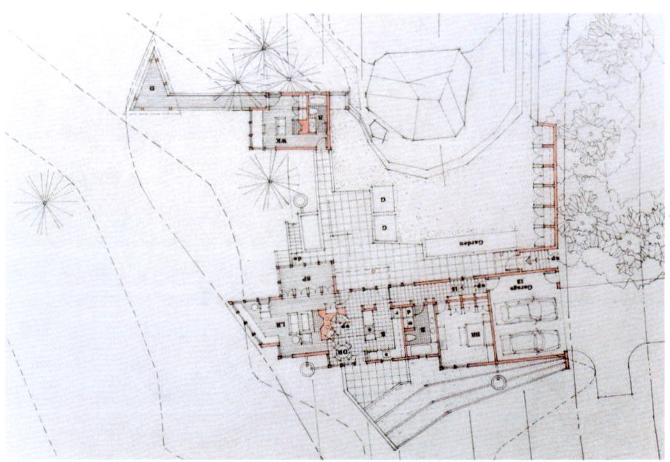

Final plan with house in courtyard enclosed by ledge

Final Model

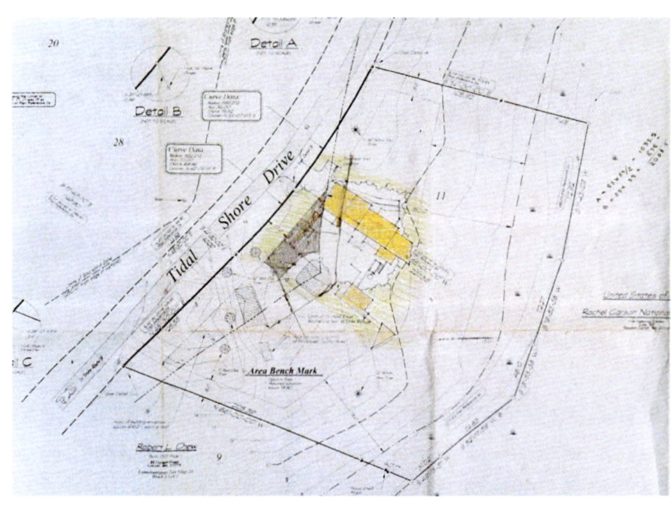

Plan of setback provided by Federal Government

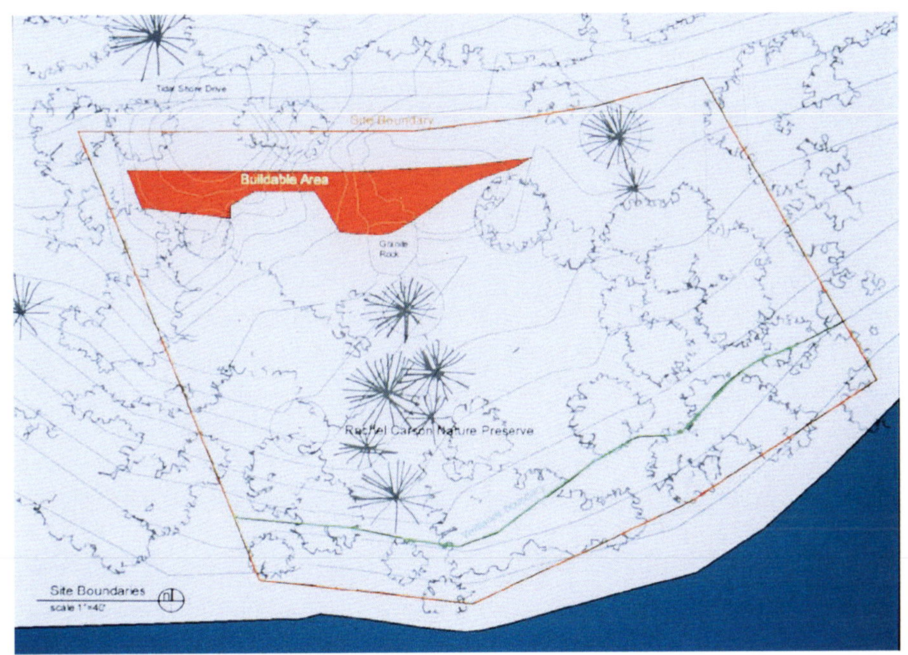

Plan of buildable area in red

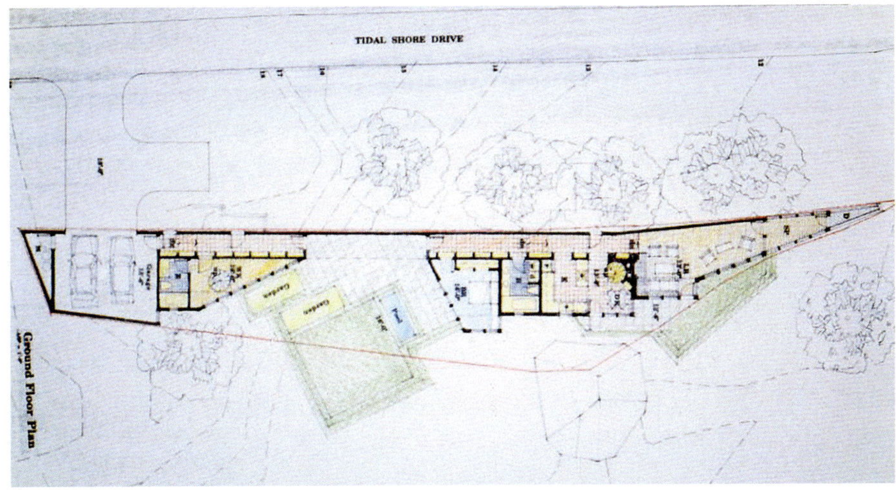

Revised plan with new setback leaving the house 18' wide by 250' long

Views of final house in winter

Stained glass window made for housewarming gift

View of length of house in fall

Detail of materials of concrete, stucco, wood and standing seam roof

Block Island Library
Block Island, R. I.

Site for project, keeping the scale of proposal to match existing houses

STOP

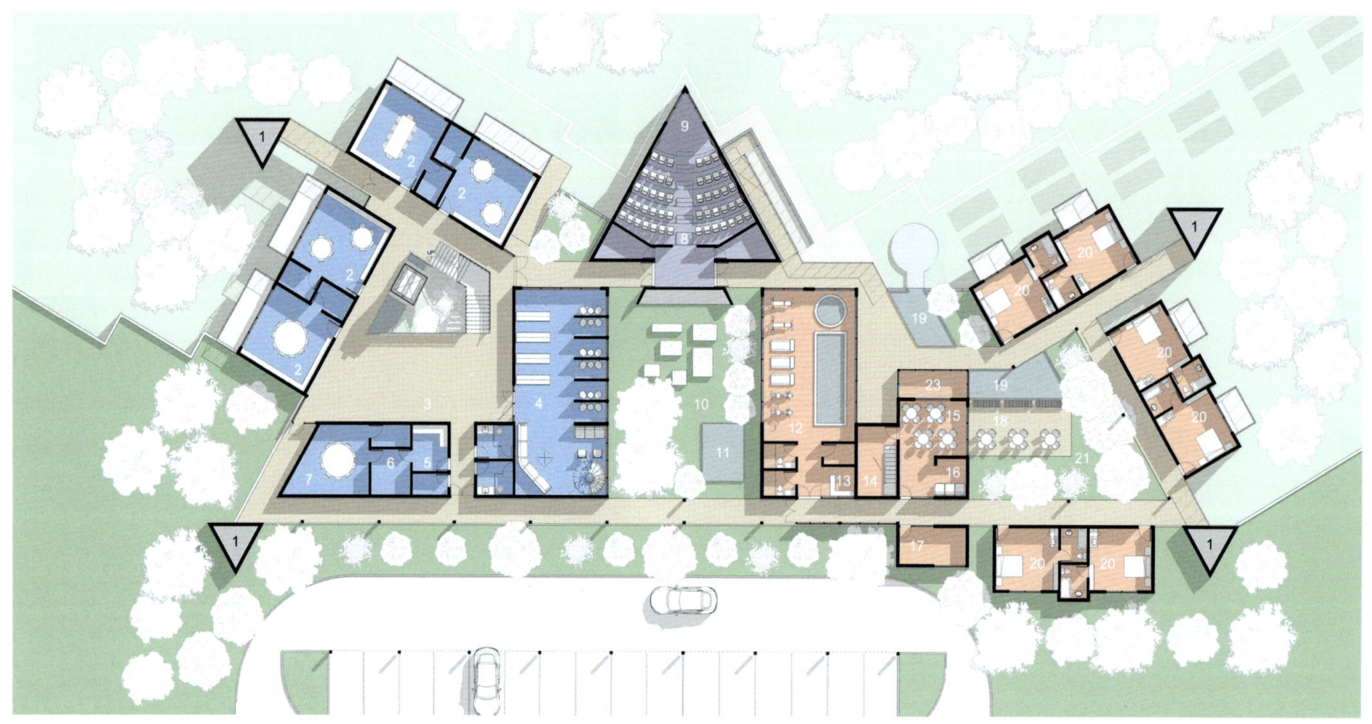

Ground Floor with Library to left and Adult Center to right

2nd Floor

Overall view of proposal

Library Ground Floor showing Art Exhibit event

Reading nooks

Typical unit for adults with small kitchen and outside balcony

Small auditorium

Dining Room and Fireplace Room

PT room with swimming pool

Children's Room

Adult Room

Courtyard with outdoor film screen

Arcade around courtyard

Fountain in Courtyard

Private courtyard of Adult Center

Oath for Architects

First proposed by Jan Wampler at public lecture on Feb. 16, 2019 to audience at the University of South Florida, School of Architecture and Community Design.

Administered to students at USF on May 4, 2019 by Jan Wampler for the first time in the US. Second giving of Oath: May 2020, USF
Third giving of Oath, May 2021, USF

Oath for Architects

On my honor, I, ______, hereby take this oath of commitment to the following principles:

To maintain the highest ethical and moral standards in my life and my architectural practice;

To commit my practice for the good of our planet and humanity;

To practice architecture according to its basic aim to provide human shelter and enriched quality of life for all humanity;

To treat clients, allied professionals inside and outside of my industry, and the general public with respect, honesty, and integrity;

To respect diverse socioeconomic identities, gender issues and rights, and to not discriminate by race, color, religion, sex, age, national origin, sexual orientation, gender identity, disability, and any other basis prohibited by law;

To strive to be an enlightened, passionate steward of both the built and the natural environments, address climate change, and conservation of Earth's natural resources;

To pass on to the next generation our responsibility to do good for the world through universal, sustainable design that meets the needs of all humankind and protects the Earth;

By taking this oath, I have accepted my duty toward the betterment of civilization, its buildings, communities, and ecosystems.

Thoughts

Monastery in Shanxi Province, China, built on side of cliff by non-architects with local materials. The ordinary becomes very extraordinary.

Monastery in Amorgos, Greece, on side of mountain by non-architects using local materials of stucco, stone and concrete by non-architects. Also becomes very extraordinary and beautiful.

Our responsibility and honor are to design an architectural echo, of joy and innocence as seen in this photo of children. This is our task.

PROPOSAL

Jan Wampler

We can never be what we can be
Till all the world
    Has
    Food
    Water
    Education
    Employment
And a home of their own

Two billion people in the world lack adequate housing, which amounts to about 20% of the world's population. I hope we as architects can begin the process of solving this terrible problem.

In 1948, Eleanor Roosevelt proposed to the United Nations a Universal Declaration of Human Rights, which included adequate housing as well as other human rights. It is now 75 years since this event, and some small endeavors toward that goal have been made, but the problem has become much more critical and is expected to increase in the next ten years. Now is the time to approach this terrible problem with a solution.

There are 200 countries in the United Nations, and there are about 200 schools of architecture in the Americas – even more if we include Asia, Europe, and Africa. If each school selected five students, then there could be least 1,000 solutions to the housing problem. Each school would be assigned a country, a client, and a site, and would be given detailed information on their clients' needs and dreams, the nature and condition of their sites, and the culture of their country and people. Then the students would have a week to ten days to sketch and design a home for their respective clients' families using local materials, to be built on a safe site free from floods, landslides, and other dangerous conditions. The parameters of the designs would be tightly controlled in terms of size of homes, ease of construction, shortness of building time, and use of sustainable local materials. Students would illustrate their designs with models, drawings, client photos, client programs, and written descriptions of their house projects, indicating materials used, reasons for these solutions, time frames for building them, and the ways in which they respond to criteria of both the limitations and the needs of the client.

The solutions would be reviewed by architects, representatives from the chosen countries, and building consultants. Awards would be given to the top 100 solutions. Then they would be exhibited at the United Nations, after which a traveling exhibition could promote the work throughout the world. A publication of all 100 solutions would be published.

Funds would be solicited to build each of the 100 solutions on a site in each country. Construction might be carried out by students, architects, faculty, contractors and clients, and each project's construction process would be documented in a film to be shown throughout the world. After the initial homes are completed, funds could be raised to build homes based on those 100 prototypes on a larger scale. Each year of a three-year plan, housing could be erected in the hope that, after three years, those two billion people would have adequate housing.

It is important to live in not only adequate housing but also a place of love to come home to and call one's own. If people have a home that they love, they are apt to strive toward better education, health, and jobs for the future.

This is my hope.

ACKNOWLEDGEMENTS

The work in this book is the result of many hours of hard labor by many people. Although I am the architect of the projects presented here, always a staff of people worked with me, to whom I am very grateful. Their dedicated work makes the designs more complete.

Over the years, many people have been that "one person" for me, who has made a difference in my career. They have always been there for me at different times in my life, always encouraging and supporting me with their ideas and thoughts. To them I am deeply grateful, as well as very fortunate.

People to thank:

People that have guided me along the way: David Isaiah Goldberg, Edwin Hannah, Karl Linn, Louis Khan, Josep Lluís Sert, Aldo Van Eyck, Fumihiko Maki, John Habraken, Ernest Kirwan, William D. Warner, David Crane, Edwin Logue, Jerzy Soltan, Jaqueline Tyrwhitt, Carlos Alvarado, Andy Anderson, Jack Myer, Donlyn Lyndon.

People that have helped me along the way: Elizabeth Reed, Kaaren Wampler, Amanda Kennedy, Todd Larson, Myron and Phyllis Rosenblum, Steven Imrich, Malcom McKenzie, Charles Norris, Paul Belliveau, Paul Lukez, Ben Wolberg, John Gasner, Steven Cooke, Robert MacLeod, Heidi Palmer, Judy Crager.

DEDICATION

For the last 13 years, I have had the honor of teaching outstanding students at the University of South Florida, School of Architecture and Community Design. They are dedicated, talented, tireless workers, and have produced some intriguing designs over the years.

This book is dedicated to them and they are listed below:

SPRING 2011

Resciniti, Emily R.
Gomez, Jose
Warner, Justin J.
Torres, Jonathan
Banks, Jordan M.
Monod, Jean-Frederic G.
Garrett, Ashley D.
Maslowski, Marcel J.
West, Brian S.
Rios, Alex M.
Deacon, Joshua D.
Roman, John
Pirozzi, Derek
Gillingham, Danelle
Morantin, Leonardo L.

SPRING 2012

Alvarez, Mary
Boyd, Nate
Cabana, Kaitlyn
Costa, Sasha Dalla
Cabana, Kaitlyn
Duran, Diana
Frye, Becky
Huller, Brennen
Jones, Nicholas
Kelmann, Stella
Kozlovsky, Jinnifer
Loper, Andrew
McDowell, Jeff
Rivera, Francarlos
Sejek, Lauren
Vereb, Billy
Wall, Matthew

SPRING 2013

Baitz, Matthew
Morra, Tyler D.
Colon, Erik
Nixon, Brianna R.
Brown, Stacey A.
Zawko, David P.
Boehmer, Hannah E.
Cano-Flores, Angie V.
Diaz, Favio C.
Gilman, James B.
Pena, Cristine
Penley, Adam D.
Santillan, Giancarlo B.
Merritt, Dustin P.
McCollum, Ann M.

SPRING 2014

Arango Lopez, Marcela
Coleman, Maeghann A.
Galbraith, Christopher B.
Larue, Leidy T.
Karakasilis, Georgina F.
Ferreira, Juan P.
Stimmel, Susan E.
Covate, Daniella M.
Stanley, Christian A.
Watts, Brian V.
Moguel, Andres M.
Plunkett, Sally
Alamo, Samuel
Dyer, Ryan L.
Powell, Jay G.
Sanchez, Israel B.

SPRING 2015

Henry, Kendrick T.
Loper Jr, Christopher S.
Henschen, Stephanie
Pilonieta, Zorth S.
Grimes, April R.
Lozano, Laura B.
Amias, Mikel
Straub, Ronald
Dominguez, Manuel H.
Alawar, Jad
Shawver, Jenna
Reynolds, Christopher A.

SPRING 2016

Marin, Vanessa
Arrubla Ruiz, Steven
Salazar Fortis, Steven G.
Garcia Mejia, Veronica R.
Vega, Yesenia
Fowke, Kimberly M.
Alai, Audrey
Rubley, Robert M.
Statzer, Victoria L.
Sportman, Bryan M.
Calderon, Laura E.
Moretta, Jorgelina
Lombana, Olga L.
Guanoluisa, Ariel
Silva, Juan

SPRING 2020

Satchwell, Matt A.
Folh, Catherine
Hernandez Romero, Luis A.
Martinez, Emily
Hasan, Bessan
Cruz, Frances A.
Cadet, Jane G.
Byron, Beltha
Vanderlaan, Jessica L.
Andrews, Amanda R.
Stefanick, Allie M.
Abuemaish, Sereen
Belizaire, Keisha

SPRING 2021

Joyce, Conor C.
Mather, Samantha L.
Chopite, Valentina
Corn, Daniel
Damiscar, Johanne
Boudreaux, Brandon
Rivera, Caleb
De La Torre, Brianne M.
Crowe, Leah G.
Guerrero Guerrero, Ramses I.
Cruz, Nayeli
McKeel, Dawson
Gascon, Nicholas G.

SPRING 2022

Gomez Pina, Paola E.
Figueiredo Botelho, Alicia
Padron, Ulises A.
Guzman, Crhistian
Cruz, Astrid
Smith, Marisa
Zreik Dos Ramos, Alan M.
Elfaki, Salma S.
Lopez Galindo, Carlos I.
Sinan, Noura
Henry, Taylor A.

SPRING 2017

Martinez, Alexander A.
Shtyrkalo, Yaroslav
Medina-Rivera, Carlos G.
Accoo, Devaughn F.
Ramos, Johnny
Langston, Jailyn F.
Nogueira, Kimberly N.
Hart, Marie W.
Gomez Gomez, Maria A.
Yanes, Natalia
Barnes, Joshua D.
Gonzalez Valero, Jose A.
Cuthbert, Robert T.

SPRING 2018

Sladden, Zackery T.
Hanna, Erik R.
Cook III, William J.
Cheng, Ana M.
Coy, Blair
Nisula, William
Ciccia, Martina
Keil, Abby
Milford, Jonathan
Correa, Zachary A.
Ribadeneira Pesantes, Emilia
Praphatsarang, Athit
Tabbalat, Mira
Meneses Prieto, Ana M.
Hirani, Nazia

SPRING 2019

Chavez, Gabriel
Pichette, Marquessa
Acosta, Elizabeth
Costello, Evan
Dampier, John
Jiang, Baibin
Le, Tran Austine B.
Martinez, Edwin
Moore, Hannah
Tran, Stella K.
White, Hunter M.
Stephanis, Jeraldy
Reed, Benjamin L.
Ramon, Mark A.
Patel, Ankita A.
Keil, Abby
Loechelt, Eric
Martinez Cruz, Antonio

SPRING 2022 (Cont'd)

Trejo Alvarez, Jenifer
Le, Thi Phuong Oanh
Britt, Anna E.
Quagliariello, Celina G.
Spence, Jose D.

SPRING 2023

Spina, Haley L.
Alkaelani, Layan
Kyaw, Phyo Hay Mar
Aldelamy, Mariam
Hollis, Kolby N.
Fernandez, Vicente R.
Le, Tinh L.
Mccarty, Kean
Bui, Andrew K.
Vivar, Lawrence

ABOUT THE AUTHOR

Jan Wampler

Photo by JT Dampier

After graduating from Harvard, GSD, in 1964, Wampler worked in San Juan, Puerto Rico as Director of Diseño Urbano at ARUV. During this time, he designed numerous housing projects and received the First Design Award in 1968 from Progressive Architecture for the project La Puntilla in the old city of San Juan. Coming back to Boston, Wampler was Director of the Planning Design Group for the Boston Redevelopment Authority. During this time, he designed the 1976 International Exposition that was to be built in Boston. In 1970 he both started an office and was asked to teach at the MIT, Architecture Program. At MIT Wampler taught till 2015 where he was Director of the Undergraduate Program. During this time, he also taught at Berkely and Pomona of the University of California as well as RISD, University of Sydney, and Tsinghua University in Beijing, China.

Wampler's office has designed many projects and received many awards with the Angela Westover House receiving Design Awards from the BSA and Massachusetts AIA.

He wrote a book entitled "All Their Own" and was featured at MIT in several exhibitions, the major one entitled "Open Strings for E", an overview of 25 years of work. Robert Campbell, an architectural critic reviewing the exhibition referred to him as the "Walt Whitman of Architecture".

Since 2010, Wampler has been a guest professor at the University of South Florida in Tampa, Florida, and finished his second book entitled "Open Notes for Young Architects" which has received numerous positive reviews.

He has several urban design and architecture projects in China. The latest is a project to design a Public Space System for Beijing, China.

Others include a Museum of Chinese Antiques, a new city for Chengdu, housing, and a community center near Beijing. In addition he has projects in Haiti, Turkey and the US with a recent project for Block Island, R.I.

He lives in Boston, MA, Block Island, RI and Gulfport, FL.

Book Credits

Jan Wampler, Architects: Steve Imrich, Nancy Agnew, Richard Page, Roger Shephley, Eric Phfier, Randoph Slaughter, Paul Lukez, John James, Gail Sullivan + more Planning Design Group, BRA. Warren Schwartz, Robert Hanna, Chu Lee, Charles North, Malcom Mckenzie, Paul Bealivuea + more. Estudio Urbano Designo / ARUV

The first foreword to this book was first written by Aldo Van Eyck for an earlier book that I wrote, entitled "Open Strings for E". This was the result of an exhibition at the MIT Museum. The second foreword was written by John Habraken for the above book and revised in 2014. The third foreword was written by Fumihiko Maki for the above book and revised in 2014. Parts of this book were taken from both *Open Strings for E* and *Open Notes of Harmony,* both printed through funds from MIT and generous donors. Other parts of this book came from talks with my students, recorded and transcripted. The work in this book that is labeled "MIT Workshop" originated in the workshops I taught in the MIT School of Architecture and Planning over many years. These were international workshops I developed to expose students to other cultures. Academic credit was given to students who enrolled in them.

Photo Credits go to Jan Wampler and Office of Jan Wampler and as noted. If not noted, source is unknown.

Oscar Riera Ojeda Publishers
Graphic Design **Juan Pablo Sarrabayrouse**
Editorial Director **Caroline Kipling**
Copy Editing **Kit Maude**

OSCAR RIERA OJEDA
PUBLISHERS

ISBN 978-1-964490-14-4
Published by Oscar Riera Ojeda Publishers Limited
Printed in China

Oscar Riera Ojeda Publishers Limited
Unit 1331, Beverley Commercial Centre, 87-105 Chatham Road South, Tsim Sha Tsui, Kowloon, Hong Kong
Production Offices
Suit 19, Shenyun Road, Nanshan District, Shenzhen 518055, China

International Customer Service & Editorial Questions: +1-484-502-5400

www.oropublishers.com | www.oscarrieraojeda.com | oscar@oscarrieraojeda.com